Swift App Development

Your First iOS App from Start to Finish

Oliver Snowden

1

2

3

Discover Other Books in the Series

"Swift Foundations: A Beginner's Guide to the Basics"

"Swift Server-Side: Introducing Swift for the Web"

"Swift Networking: Building Apps that Connect"

"Swift Security: Building Safe and Secure Apps"

"Swift for DevOps: Automating Development Workflows"

"Swift for Cloud Services: Integrating with AWS, Azure, Google Cloud and Firebase"

"Swift for Cloud-Native Development: Leveraging Kubernetes and Docker"

"Swift for IoT: Building Applications for Connected Devices"

"Swift for Artificial Intelligence: Developing AI-Powered Applications"

"Swift for Artificial Intelligence: Developing AI-Powered Applications"

"Swift for Virtual Reality: Building Augmented and AR/VR Experiences"

Disclaimer

Swift App Development: Your First iOS App from Start to Finish by Oliver Snowden is intended for educational and informational purposes only. The content within this book is designed to provide guidance and insights into the process of developing iOS applications using Swift.

While every effort has been made to ensure the accuracy and completeness of the information presented, the author and publisher assume no responsibility for any errors, omissions, or inaccuracies.

Readers are encouraged to use their discretion and consult with a professional for specific advice tailored to their individual circumstances.

Introduction

Welcome to **"Swift App Development: Your First iOS App from Start to Finish"**—your gateway to the exciting world of iOS app development! If you've ever dreamed of creating your own apps but felt overwhelmed about where to start, you're in the right place. This book was created specifically for beginners like you who are eager to learn Swift and build functional, polished iOS applications from scratch.

Imagine holding your iPhone and proudly showcasing an app that you created. The journey from a simple idea to a fully functional app might seem daunting, but with the right guidance and a bit of perseverance, you can turn that dream into reality. That's where this book comes in.

In **Swift App Development: Your First iOS App from Start to Finish**, we will guide you step-by-step through the entire process of developing your first iOS app using Swift, Apple's powerful and intuitive programming language. You'll learn the fundamentals of Swift, grasp essential concepts of iOS development, and gain hands-on experience through practical exercises and real-world examples.

We'll begin by introducing the Swift programming language, covering its syntax, basic functions, and core principles. You'll quickly gain confidence as you write your first lines of Swift code.

Next, we'll dive into Xcode, Apple's integrated development environment (IDE). You'll learn how to navigate Xcode, set up your project, and use its powerful tools to streamline your development process.

A great app starts with a great user interface. We'll guide you through the process of designing your app's UI, using Interface Builder to create visually appealing and user-friendly layouts.

With your UI in place, it's time to bring your app to life. You'll learn how to connect your UI elements to your code, handle user interactions, and implement key functionalities that make your app unique.

Chapter 1: Swift and iOS Development

At the heart of iOS development lies Swift, a powerful and intuitive programming language designed by Apple to simplify the process of building robust applications for iPhone, iPad, and beyond. In this chapter, we will explore the fundamental concepts of Swift, the significance of iOS development, and the essentials of getting started in this vibrant ecosystem.

1.1 The Rise of iOS Development

Since its launch in 2007, the iOS platform has garnered a vast user base, with millions of active devices around the globe. This success is not just by chance; Apple has cultivated a committed developer community and embraced a philosophy of continuous improvement. The App Store, launched in 2008, revolutionized the way software is distributed and monetized, creating an exciting market for developers to showcase their skills and creativity.

The demand for high-quality applications continues to grow, with iOS devices dominating the high-end market segment. Businesses and entrepreneurs are increasingly tapping into this potential, leading to opportunities for developers who can leverage Apple's extensive ecosystem. The iOS platform offers an exceptional blend of performance, security, and user experience, making it an attractive arena for budding developers and seasoned professionals alike.

1.2 Why Learn Swift?

Swift, introduced in 2014, represents a significant shift in how applications for Apple platforms are developed. Designed as a modern programming language, Swift is approachable and powerful, making it ideal for beginners and experienced developers. Here are a few compelling reasons to learn Swift:

1.2.1 Modern and Readable Syntax

Swift features a clean and expressive syntax that eliminates much of the boilerplate code required in previous languages like Objective-C. This improves readability and simplifies the learning process. Swift allows developers to express ideas more clearly, leading to a more enjoyable coding experience.

1.2.2 Safety and Performance

Swift is built with safety in mind, reducing common programming errors. Features like optionals, automatic reference counting, and strong typing help ensure that errors can be caught at compile time rather than runtime. Additionally, Swift is designed to be fast, providing performance improvements that leverage the capabilities of Apple's hardware.

1.2.3 Interactive Development

The introduction of Playgrounds in Xcode allows developers to experiment and prototype code in real-time. This interactive environment encourages exploration and learning, making it accessible for beginners to tinker with code without the need for a full-blown application.

1.2.4 Strong Community and Ecosystem

Swift has quickly gained traction, and a vibrant community has formed around it. With numerous libraries,frameworks, and resources available, developers can find support, tutorials, and tools to aid their learning journey. Open-source contributions have further enriched the ecosystem, fostering collaboration and innovation.

1.3 The iOS Development Process

Developing an iOS application can be broken down into several stages, each requiring unique skills andknowledge. Understanding this process is crucial for new developers. Here's a brief overview of the keysteps involved:

1.3.1 Planning

Every successful application begins with a well-thought-out plan. This includes defining the app's purpose,target audience, features, and user experience. Prototyping ideas through wireframes can help visualize the concept and refine the overall vision.

1.3.2 Development

Once planning is complete, the development phase begins. Using Xcode, Apple's integrated development environment (IDE), developers will write code in Swift to implement the app's functionality. This stage alsoincludes creating user interfaces using SwiftUI or UIKit, as well as integrating any necessary libraries and frameworks.

1.3.3 Testing

Testing is a critical part of the development cycle. Developers must ensure that their application functions correctly and is free of bugs. Various testing methodologies, such as unit tests and UI testing, can help identify issues before the app is released to users.

1.3.4 Deployment

Once the app has been tested and refined, it's time for deployment. Developers submit their apps to the App Store, where they will undergo Apple's review process. If approved, the app will be available for download, marking the culmination of the development effort.

1.3.5 Maintenance and Updates

The work doesn't end once the app is live. Regular updates are necessary to fix bugs, improve performance, and introduce new features. Engaging with user feedback and analytics can help guide future developments and enhancements.

1.4 Getting Started

As with any endeavor, the first step is often the hardest. However, the path to becoming an iOS developer has never been more accessible. Here are some steps to guide you on your journey:

Set Up Your Environment: Download Xcode, Apple's IDE for creating iOS applications. It includes everything you need to build, test, and submit apps to the App Store.

Learn the Basics of Swift: Familiarize yourself with Swift's syntax, data types, control flow, and functions. Online resources, books, and courses are plentiful and can help you get started.

Understand iOS Fundamentals: Study the core concepts of iOS development, including the Model-View-Controller (MVC) design pattern, user interface design with UIKit or SwiftUI, and network programming.

Build Projects: Apply what you've learned by creating small applications. Practical experience is vital in solidifying your understanding and developing your skills.

Engage with the Community: Participate in forums, attend local meetups or online workshops, and connect with other developers. Sharing knowledge and experiences can significantly accelerate your learning.

The journey into Swift and iOS development offers vast opportunities for creativity and innovation. As you embark on this exciting path, remember that perseverance and practice are key.

The power of Swift for programming

Introduced by Apple in 2014, Swift is designed to be both powerful and easy to use, aiming to give developers a robust language that enhances productivity while ensuring safety and performance. This chapter delves into the unique features that make Swift a compelling choice for programmers, explores its impact on software development, and reflects on its future in the programming world.

A Modern Language for Modern Development

Swift draws inspiration from multiple programming languages, combining the best features of Objective-C, Python, Ruby, and others. This synthesis results in a modern programming language that emphasizes simplicity and efficiency. The syntax in Swift is concise and expressive, making it not only easy to read but also straightforward to write. For instance, concepts such as optionals, type inference, and closures are integrated seamlessly into the language, allowing developers to write less code that is easier to debug.

1. Safety First: Type Safety and Memory Management

One of Swift's most lauded features is its strong emphasis on safety. Type safety helps catch errors at compile time rather than at runtime, minimizing the chances of crashes and bugs in production. Swift requires developers to specify data types, and its optionals system allows for the safe handling of nil values. This feature prevents common pitfalls such as null pointer exceptions, which have plagued many other programming languages.

Moreover, Swift employs Automatic Reference Counting (ARC) to manage memory, ensuring that memory leaks are kept to a minimum. Developers can focus on writing code rather than worrying about manual memory management, which is especially beneficial in large-scale applications where resource efficiency iscritical.

2. Performance and Efficiency

Swift boasts performance akin to C-based languages while offering higher-level abstractions that reduce development time. The Swift compiler is optimized for speed, making Swift applications perform well, whether they are simple utilities or complex systems. Features like value types, which allow objects to be copied rather than referenced, contribute to performance enhancements and promote safety, as they eliminate the need for synchronization in many cases.

Additionally, Swift's interoperability with Objective-C allows developers to use existing codebases and libraries while gradually transitioning to Swift. This feature provides flexibility and marks a large advantagefor legacy projects, minimizing disruption during the adoption of new technologies.

3. A Rich Ecosystem and Community

The growth of Swift is bolstered by a robust ecosystem and an enthusiastic developer community. The availability of numerous frameworks such as SwiftUI for UI design, Combine for reactive programming, and CoreML for machine learning applications enhances the versatility of Swift. Furthermore, the Swift PackageManager simplifies the process of managing dependencies, making it easier for developers to integrate libraries and frameworks into their projects.

The community around Swift is vibrant and actively contributes resources, libraries, and tools that facilitate development. Online forums, Swift user groups, and conferences provide valuable spaces for learning and collaboration, ensuring that developers stay updated with the latest best practices and innovations.

4. Cross-Platform Development

Swift has evolved beyond its initial confines of Apple platforms. Swift's open-source nature means that it is now available for various platforms, including Linux and Windows. This expansion opens up new possibilities for developers who wish to leverage Swift for server-side applications, system programming, and cross-platform app development. Tools like Vapor and Perfect enable backend development in Swift, broadening its applicability.

Moreover, Swift for TensorFlow is an ambitious project that explores the potential of Swift in the machine learning space, further signifying the language's versatility and relevance in modern programming paradigms.

The power of Swift lies not only in its modern syntax and advanced safety features but also in its vision for the future of programming. As the demand for high-performance applications grows, Swift's ability to combine speed, safety, and ease of use makes it an attractive choice for developers. With its expanding ecosystem, vibrant community, and cross-platform capabilities, Swift is poised to remain a significant playerin the programming landscape for years to come.

Understanding Develop for iOS

Apple's iOS is a robust operating system powering a vast array of devices, from iPhones and iPads to AppleTVs. The iOS ecosystem provides a unique opportunity to create powerful applications that can reach a global audience, and this chapter will lay the foundation for understanding the essentials of developing for this platform.

1.1 Overview of iOS Development

iOS development refers to the process of creating applications for devices that run on Apple's iOS. This development is centered around several key components:

Programming Languages: The primary languages used in iOS development are Swift and Objective-C.Swift, introduced by Apple in 2014, has quickly become the preferred choice due to its simplicity and modern features, while Objective-C remains crucial for maintaining legacy applications.

Development Environment: The official integrated development environment (IDE) for iOS development is Xcode. It provides all the necessary tools, including a code editor, interface builder, anddebugging tools.

Frameworks and APIs: iOS developers utilize a vast array of frameworks and Application Programming Interfaces (APIs) provided by Apple, such as UIKit for user interface components, Core Data for data management, and SwiftUI for declarative UI programming.

App Distribution: Understanding how to distribute your app through the App Store is critical, including the submission process, app review guidelines, and monetization strategies.

1.2 The iOS Ecosystem

The iOS ecosystem is characterized by a dynamic and diverse community of users and developers. With more than a billion active iOS devices worldwide, developers have access to a massive audience. Below are some essential aspects of the iOS ecosystem:

1.2.1 Target Audience

Knowing your target audience is essential for developing successful applications. iOS users tend to prioritize quality and design; thus, providing a seamless user experience is crucial. Understanding demographics, user behavior, and preferences can help tailor your app to meet the needs of your audience.

1.2.2 Design Guidelines

Apple places significant importance on user interface (UI) and user experience (UX) design. The Human Interface

Guidelines (HIG) provide a comprehensive outline of designing intuitive and beautiful apps.
Utilizing design principles such as clarity, deference, and depth can set your app apart in the competitive iOS market.

1.2.3 App Monetization Strategies

Developers can choose various monetization strategies, including in-app purchases, subscriptions, ads, or paid downloads. Selecting the right model often depends on the app's audience and functionality. For instance, a free app with in-app purchases might attract a larger audience, while a niche app could benefit

from a one-time purchase model.

1.3 Getting Started with Development

1.3.1 Setting Up the Development Environment

Before diving into coding, you must set up Xcode on your macOS machine. The following steps summarize the setup:

Download Xcode: Install Xcode from the Mac App Store or the Apple Developer website.
Create a Developer Account: You'll need an Apple Developer account to test on real devices and deploy apps.
Familiarize Yourself with Xcode: Explore the project navigator, editor, interface builder, and simulator to get comfortable with the environment.

1.3.2 Learning Swift

Swift is a modern, user-friendly programming language. Beginners should focus on understanding the basics:

Syntax: Learn the structure of Swift code, including variables, constants, data types, and operators.
Control Flow: Understand how to use conditionals (if/else statements) and loops (for, while) for flow control.
Functions and Closures: Grasp how to declutter code by using functions and their closures for callbacks and asynchronous tasks.

Swift's official documentation, along with numerous online tutorials, offers a rich resource for learning the language.

1.4 Building Your First iOS App

To solidify your understanding, let's outline the core steps to create a simple iOS app: ### 1.4.1 Create a New Xcode Project
Open Xcode and create a new project.
Choose the 'App' template and specify your target device (iPhone or iPad).
Set up your project name and organizational settings. ### 1.4.2 Design the User Interface
Utilize the Interface Builder to drag and drop UI elements like labels, buttons, and text fields onto your main view.
Connect UI elements to your code using IBOutlet (to reference UI components) and IBAction (to handle user actions).

1.4.3 Implementing Logic

Write Swift code to handle user interactions and implement functionalities.
Utilize APIs and frameworks to enhance the app's features, such as networking or data storage. ### 1.4.4 Testing Your App
Use the Xcode simulator to test your app's functionality.
If you have a physical device, deploy your app to test its performance and behavior in a real-world environment.

Understanding iOS development is more than just mastering technical skills; it involves grasping the ecosystem, user expectations, and design principles. With the right foundation in place, you can embark on a journey to create applications that cater to a global audience, bringing innovative solutions and delightful experiences to users.

Chapter 2: Setting Up Your Development Environment

A well-configured environment not only enhances your productivity but also helps you get acquainted with the tools and practices of modern software development. In this chapter, we will guide you through the process of setting up your development environment for Swift.

2.1 Choosing Your Development Environment

The first step in setting up your Swift development environment is choosing the right IDE (Integrated Development Environment) or text editor. While several options are available, the two most popular choices for Swift development are **Xcode** and **Visual Studio Code**.

2.1.1 Xcode

Xcode is Apple's official IDE for macOS and is the most comprehensive tool for Swift development, especially for building applications for iOS, macOS, watchOS, and tvOS. Here's why you might consider using Xcode:

Feature-Rich: Xcode comes with everything you need to develop applications, including Interface Builder for UI design, a powerful code editor with autocomplete suggestions, and built-in debugging tools.
Swift Playgrounds: Xcode includes a feature called

Playgrounds, which allows you to write Swift code and see the results immediately, making it a great tool for experimenting with new concepts and functionalities.
Swift Package Manager: Xcode integrates seamlessly with the Swift Package Manager, making dependency management straightforward.

Installing XcodeTo install Xcode:
Open the Mac App Store.
Search for "Xcode."
Click on the "Get" button to download and install it.
Once installed, launch Xcode and complete the initial setup process.### 2.1.2 Visual Studio Code
If you are looking for a more lightweight solution or if you plan to use Swift for server-side applications,
Visual Studio Code (VS Code) is an excellent choice. Here are some reasons to consider it:

Cross-Platform: VS Code runs on macOS, Windows, and Linux, making it versatile for different development environments.
Customization: With a vast library of extensions, you can tailor VS Code to suit your workflow perfectly.
Integrated Terminal: It provides a built-in terminal, making it easy to run Swift commands directly from your IDE.

Installing Visual Studio Code

To install Visual Studio Code:

Go to the [Visual Studio Code website](https://code.visualstudio.com/).
Download the correct version for your operating system.
Follow the installation instructions provided on the website.

Once installed, you will want to install some extensions to enhance your Swift development experience:

Swift Language Support: Install an extension that offers syntax highlighting and code completion for Swift.
CodeLLDB: If you require debugging capabilities, consider installing the CodeLLDB extension. ## 2.2 Installing the Swift Toolchain
Regardless of which IDE you choose, you'll need to ensure that the Swift toolchain is installed on your machine. The toolchain includes the Swift compiler and standard library necessary for building Swift applications.

2.2.1 macOS Installation

If you are using macOS and have installed Xcode, the Swift toolchain is already included. To verify your installation, open the terminal and type:

```bash
swift --version
```

You should see output indicating the version of Swift that is installed.### 2.2.2 Linux Installation

For Linux users, you will need to install the Swift toolchain separately. Here's how you can do this:

Visit the [official Swift website](https://swift.org/download/) and select the appropriate version for your distribution.
Follow the installation instructions provided on the site for your specific Linux distribution (Debian, Ubuntu, CentOS, etc.).

After installation, verify it in the terminal:

```bash
swift --version
```

2.2.3 Windows Installation

Swift is still in the early stages of support for Windows, but you can set up your environment by following these steps:

Download the latest Swift build for Windows from the [official Swift website](https://swift.org/download/).
Extract the downloaded archive and add the `bin` directory to your system's PATH.
Open Command Prompt and verify the installation:

```bash
swift --version
```

2.3 Setting Up Your First Project

25

Now that your development environment is set up, the next step is to create your first Swift project. ### 2.3.1 Creating a Project in Xcode
Open Xcode and select "Create a new Xcode project."
Choose a template (e.g., Command Line Tool) and click "Next."
Fill in the project details (product name, team, organization, etc.).
Select Swift as the language and choose a location to save your project.
Click "Create" to generate your project.

2.3.2 Creating a Project in Visual Studio Code

Open Visual Studio Code.
Create a new folder for your project.
Open the terminal (View > Terminal).
Run the following command to create a new Swift package:

```bash
swift package init --type executable
```

This command sets up a new Swift package complete with the directory structure and a simple "Hello, World!" program.

2.4 Configuring Version Control

As you begin to code, using a version control system like **Git** is essential. It allows you to track changes, collaborate with others, and maintain a history of your project.

2.4.1 Setting Up GitTo set up Git:
Install Git if you haven't already. You can download it from the [Git website](https://git-scm.com/).
Initialize a Git repository in your project folder by running:

```bash
git init
```

Create a `.gitignore` file to exclude files that should not be tracked, such as build artifacts or user-specific settings. You can find Swift-specific .gitignore templates online.

2.4.2 Making Your First Commit

Once you've made changes to your project files, you can commit them to Git:

```bash
git add .

git commit -m "Initial commit"
```

Setting up your development environment is a foundational step on your journey to becoming proficient with Swift. Whether you choose Xcode for its comprehensive features or Visual Studio Code for its flexibility, the tools you configure will significantly impact your development experience.

Installing Xcode in Swift

With support for Swift programming, it provides developers with powerful tools for code editing, debugging, UI design, and project management. This chapter will guide you through the steps required to install Xcode, ensuring you're prepared to start developing in Swift.

System Requirements

Before diving into the installation process, it's essential to ensure your Mac meets the necessary requirements for running Xcode:

Operating System: Xcode requires macOS to run. Always ensure that your macOS is updated to the latest version that supports the version of Xcode you are planning to install.

Storage: Xcode requires significant storage space. Be sure to have at least 10-20 GB of free disk space for a proper installation, as well as additional space for projects and resources.

Hardware: While older Macs may run Xcode, it supports the latest hardware to utilize all features and optimizations efficiently.

Check Apple's official documentation for specific version requirements and ensure your Mac meets them. ## Installing Xcode

Step 1: Access the Mac App Store

Open the **App Store** application on your Mac. You can find it by clicking on the App Store icon in the Dock or by searching for "App Store" using Spotlight (Cmd + Space).

In the search bar, type "Xcode" and hit Enter. You will be presented with the Xcode application in the search results.

Step 2: Download Xcode

Click on the **Xcode** icon from the search results.

Once you are on the Xcode page, click on the **Get** button (or the cloud icon if you have previously downloaded it). If prompted, enter your Apple ID and password to start the download process.

The download can take some time depending on your internet speed, so be patient as Xcode is a large application.

Step 3: Install Xcode

After the download is complete, the installation process will begin automatically. If it doesn't start, navigate to your **Applications** folder in Finder and locate the Xcode app.

Double-click on the Xcode application to begin the installation. You might be prompted to accept the terms and conditions; do so to continue.

The installation will proceed and may take a few minutes. Once it is finished, Xcode will be available in your Applications folder.

Step 4: Launch Xcode

Open the Applications folder and find **Xcode**. Double-click to launch it.

Upon launching for the first time, Xcode may prompt you to install additional components. Make sure to allow this process as it helps enable all features of the IDE.

You may also receive a dialog box indicating that Xcode requires permissions to access specific resources like the Developer folder. Grant these permissions to ensure optimal functionality.

Initial Setup

Upon first launch, you might want to go through a few initial setup steps:

Choose a Development Environment: Xcode asks whether you want to use different templates for app development. You can either choose the latest SwiftUI template or UIKit templates depending on your needs.

Explore the Interface: Familiarize yourself with the Xcode environment. The workspace window is where you will spend most of your time coding, debugging, and testing your applications.

Create a New Project: You can create your first Swift project by selecting "Create a new Xcode project" from the welcome dialog. Choose a template that suits your app idea, specify product details like the name and organization identifier, and select Swift as the programming language.

Setting Up Command Line Tools

To utilize Xcode's powerful command line capabilities, you need to install the Command Line Tools:

Open **Xcode** and navigate to `Xcode` in the menu bar.

Select **Preferences**, then click on the **Locations** tab.

Under the "Command Line Tools" dropdown, select the latest version of Xcode available. This will ensure that you can use Swift and Xcode-compatible tools in the terminal.

Congratulations! You have successfully installed Xcode and are ready to start your journey in Swift development. As you become familiar with the environment, take time to explore the IDE's features, such as the debugging tools, Interface Builder, and the Swift Playgrounds for testing your Swift code. In the upcoming chapters, we will dive deeper into Swift programming, starting with the fundamentals and advancing toward building complete applications. Happy coding!

Understanding Xcode Interface in Swift

As the primary tool for developing applications for iOS, macOS, watchOS, and tvOS, understanding the Xcode interface is crucial for any Swift developer. In this chapter, we will delve into the various components of the Xcode interface, explore its features, and offer insights into how to maximize efficiency while developing Swift applications.

1. Introduction to Xcode

When you launch Xcode for the first time, you are greeted with a clean, intuitive interface that provides access to all the essential features you will need for software development. Xcode is designed to help developers create high-quality applications through its powerful features, including code editing, debugging, version control, and interface design.

1.1 Overview of the Xcode Interface

The main components of the Xcode interface include:

Navigator Area: Located on the left side, the Navigator Area provides quick access to your files, symbols, search results, and more.

Editor Area: The Editor Area is where you write your Swift code. This area also supports Interface Builder for designing user interfaces visually.

Toolbar: The Toolbar at the top offers essential

controls such as Run, Stop, and access to various build settings.

Utilities Area: On the right side, the Utilities Area provides inspectors and libraries that allowdevelopers to adjust properties and access resources like images, colors, and more.

Debug Area: At the bottom, the Debug Area displays information about the running application, including console logs, variable values, and the debugger controls.

Let's take a closer look at these components. ## 2. The Navigator Area
The Navigator Area is pivotal for managing your files and code. It consists of several navigators:

Project Navigator: Displays all files in your project. You can organize your files into groups and navigate through your project structure easily.

Symbol Navigator: Lists all the symbols (classes, methods, etc.) in your project. This section isinvaluable for quick navigation and code comprehension.

Search Navigator: Allows you to search for keywords, files, and symbols within your project. This feature is especially useful for larger projects.

Issue Navigator: Displays errors and warnings in your code. This navigator aids in identifying and resolving issues quickly.

Debug Navigator: Provides information related to app performance during debugging, such as memory usage and CPU load.

3. The Editor Area

The Editor Area is where the magic happens. Here, you will spend most of your time writing Swift code and creating user interfaces. The Editor Area can display different types of content:

Code Editor: When you open a Swift file, you will see the code editor, which features syntax highlighting, code completion, and error checking. You can split the editor to view multiple files simultaneously.

Interface Builder: For UI design, Xcode integrates Interface Builder directly into the Editor Area. Here, you can visually design the layout of your app using storyboards and Auto Layout.

Version Editor: This allows you to compare different versions of your code when using version control, helping you manage changes effectively.

4. The Utilities Area

Situated on the right, the Utilities Area holds two key components:

Inspectors: Here, you can view and edit properties of your selected object, whether it's a UI component in Interface Builder or a piece of code. There are multiple

34

inspectors, including the Attributes Inspector and Size Inspector, helping streamline customizations.

Library: The library contains UI elements, code snippets, and other resources you can drag and dropinto your project. Libraries include standard UI components, design assets, and global code snippets that enhance development speed.

5. The Toolbar

The Toolbar is your command center while working in Xcode. It consists of several buttons and dropdownmenus for quick access to actions:

Run Button: This button compiles your code and runs your application on a simulator or connecteddevice.

Stop Button: Stops the running application.

Scheme Selector: Choose the scheme which specifies the environment (like app target and device) inwhich the app will run.

Device Selector: Select the iOS simulator or connected device you want to use for testing yourapplication.

6. The Debug Area

The Debug Area is where you can inspect your app's behavior and troubleshoot issues. It includes:

Console Output: Displays logs and print statements,

helping you track application behavior and diagnose problems.

Variable View: Allows you to see the values of variables during runtime, enabling you to inspect the state of your application while debugging.

Debug Controls: Provides buttons for stepping through your code, pausing execution, and viewing stack traces.

7. Tips for Efficient Use of Xcode

Keyboard Shortcuts: Familiarizing yourself with keyboard shortcuts can significantly speed up your workflow. For example, Command + N opens a new file, while Command + B builds the project.

Customizing the Interface: Xcode allows you to rearrange or hide various areas to suit your workflow. Take advantage of this flexibility.

Swift Playgrounds: Use Swift Playgrounds to test snippets of Swift code quickly without creating a full project. This can be particularly useful for prototyping.

Documentation: Xcode provides built-in access to Apple's documentation. Use it to understand Swift functions and libraries better.

Version Control: Integrate Git within Xcode to manage your code versions effectively, allowing for better collaboration and tracking of changes.

Understanding the Xcode interface is a fundamental step in becoming proficient in Swift development. The various components, from the Navigator Area to the Debug Area, are designed to work together seamlessly, enabling developers to write, debug, and manage their applications efficiently.

Chapter 3: Swift Basics

Swift is designed to work with Apple's Cocoa and Cocoa Touch frameworks, making it the primary language for iOS, macOS, watchOS, and tvOS development. Whether you're a beginner or an experienced developer looking to expand your skills, this chapter will provide you with the foundational knowledge you need to start coding in Swift.

3.1 Getting Started with Swift

Before we dive deep into the language, let's briefly discuss how to set up your environment. You can write Swift code in various environments such as Xcode, which is Apple's integrated development environment (IDE) for macOS, or using online Swift playgrounds. Xcode provides a rich suite of tools to help you develop and test your applications.

3.1.1 Setting Up Xcode
Download Xcode: If you haven't installed Xcode yet, you can download it from the Mac App Store.
Creating a New Project: Launch Xcode, select "Create a new Xcode project," and follow the prompts to set up your first Swift project.
Exploring Swift Playgrounds: For beginners, Swift Playgrounds is an excellent way to experiment with Swift code interactively. It's a fun and engaging way to learn the basics.

3.2 Swift Syntax and Structure

Swift's syntax is clean and expressive, making it easy to

read and write. Let's break down some of the core elements of Swift syntax.

3.2.1 Variables and Constants

In Swift, you can declare variables and constants using the `var` and `let` keywords, respectively.

```swift
var name = "John Doe" // A variable that can be changed
let age = 30   // A constant that cannot be changed
```

Variables (`var`) are used for values that can change throughout the program.
Constants (`let`) are used for values that remain constant once set.### 3.2.2 Data Types
Swift supports various data types, including:

String: Textual data
Int: Whole numbers
Double: Decimal numbers
Bool: Boolean values (true or false) Here's how you can declare them:
```swift
let greeting: String = "Hello, World!"

var temperature: Double = 72.5var isRaining: Bool = false
```

3.2.3 Control Flow

Swift provides control flow statements like `if`, `else`,

39

`switch`, and loops to execute code conditionally or repetitively.

If Statement

```swift
let score = 85

if score >= 90 { print("Grade: A")
} else if score >= 80 {print("Grade: B")
} else { print("Grade: C")
}
```

Switch Statement

```swift
let number = 2

switch number {case 1:
print("One")case 2:
print("Two")case 3:
print("Three")default:
print("Not 1, 2, or 3")
}
```

Loops

You can use `for` and `while` loops for iteration.

```swift
for i in 1...5 {
```

```
print(i) // Prints numbers from 1 to 5
}

var count = 5 while count > 0 {
print(count)count -= 1
}
```

```
```

3.3 Functions

Functions are reusable blocks of code that perform a specific task. They can accept parameters and return values.

```swift
func greet(person: String) -> String { return "Hello, \(person)!"
}

let greetingMessage = greet(person: "Alice")
print(greetingMessage) // Prints "Hello, Alice!"
```

3.4 Collections

Swift provides powerful collection types, including arrays, dictionaries, and sets.### 3.4.1 Arrays
An array is a list of values of the same type:

```swift
var fruits: [String] = ["Apple", "Banana", "Cherry"]
fruits.append("Orange") // Adding an item to the array
```

3.4.2 Dictionaries

A dictionary stores key-value pairs:

```swift
```

```swift
var ages: [String: Int] = ["Alice": 30, "Bob": 25]
ages["Charlie"] = 28 // Adding a new key-value pair
```

3.4.3 Sets

A set is a collection of unique values:

```swift
var numbers: Set<Int> = [1, 2, 3, 4, 5]
numbers.insert(3) // Inserting a duplicate value has no effect
```

3.5 Error Handling

Error handling in Swift is done using `do-catch` blocks. You can throw and catch errors as needed.

```swift
enum SampleError: Error { case somethingWentWrong
}

func riskyFunction() throws {
throw SampleError.somethingWentWrong
}

do {
try riskyFunction()
} catch {
print("Caught an error: \(error)")
}
```

In this chapter, we've covered the basics of Swift, including its syntax, control flow, data types, functions, and error handling. By understanding these fundamental concepts, you're well on your way to becoming proficient in Swift programming. In the coming chapters, we'll dive deeper into more advanced topics, including object-oriented programming, closures, and working with the iOS SDK. Keep practicing, and soon you'll be creating amazing applications!

Variables and Constants in Swift

Two fundamental concepts in any programming language are variables and constants. Understanding how to use these constructs wisely will empower you to write cleaner, more efficient Swift code.

What are Variables?

In Swift, a variable is a named storage location in memory that can hold different values over time. Variables are created using the `var` keyword. This means that you can change the value of a variable after its initial definition.

Syntax

Here's the basic syntax for creating a variable:

```swift
var variableName: DataType = initialValue
```

```
` ` `
```

`var` is the keyword that indicates you are declaring a variable.
`variableName` is the name you choose for your variable. It should be descriptive to help others (and yourself!) understand its purpose.
`DataType` specifies the type of data the variable will store (like `Int`, `String`, `Double`, etc.).
`initialValue` is the value assigned to the variable at the time of declaration.### Example

```swift
var age: Int = 30
var name: String = "Alice" var salary: Double = 75000.50
```

In this example, `age` is a variable that holds an integer value, `name` holds a string, and `salary` is a variable for a double value representing a salary amount.

Updating Variables

You can update the value of a variable any number of times:

```swift
age = 31
name = "Bob"
```

It's important to note that when you change the value of a variable, you do not need to re-declare the datatype, as Swift automatically knows the type from the initial definition.

What are Constants?

A constant, on the other hand, is a named storage location in memory that, once initialized, cannot be changed throughout its lifespan in the code. Constants are declared using the `let` keyword. This makes them particularly useful for values that should remain constant or immutable, enhancing code safety and readability. ### Syntax
Similar to variables, the syntax for defining a constant is:

```swift
let constantName: DataType = initialValue
```

`let` denotes that the value is a constant.
The rest of the structure is similar to that of variables. ### Example
```swift
let pi: Double = 3.14159
let maximumScore: Int = 100
let greeting: String = "Hello, World!"
```

In this example, `pi`, `maximumScore`, and `greeting` are constants. Once their values are assigned, they cannot be altered.

Attempting to Change a Constant

If you try to change the value of a constant after declaration, Swift will generate an error:

```swift
greeting = "Hello, Swift!" // This will cause a compile-time error
```

Type Inference and Explicit Declaration

Swift is designed with type inference, meaning it can deduce the type of variable or constant from the value assigned without needing explicit type declaration. This feature allows for more concise and clearer code.

Example of Type InferenceYou can simply write:
```swift
var height = 5.9
let isSwiftFun = true
```

In this case, `height` is inferred to be a `Double`, and `isSwiftFun` is inferred to be a `Bool` withoutexplicitly stating their types.

Best Practices

Use Constants When Possible: If you know that a value will not change, define it as a constant using `let`. This will help prevent accidental modifications and make your code more predictable.

Prefer Descriptive Names: Whether you are defining a variable or a constant, always use clear and descriptive names. For example, instead of `v`, use `userAge`.

Follow Naming Conventions: In Swift, it's conventional to use camelCase for variable and constant names. For example, use `firstName` instead of `FirstName`.

Group Related Variables: Consider grouping related variables and constants together for easier readability. For instance, grouping user-related information in a struct.

Understanding the distinction between variables and constants in Swift is an essential building block for writing effective Swift code. By knowing when to use `var` and `let`, you can create programs that are not only functional but also clear and maintainable.

Data Types and Operators in Swift

Central to the efficiency and readability of Swift is its robust system of data types and operators. In this chapter, we will explore the foundational data types available in Swift and how operators work with them.

Understanding Data Types

Data types are essential in any programming language as they define the type of data that can be stored and manipulated. Swift has a rich set of built-in data types that can be categorized into two main groups: **value types** and **reference types**.

Value Types

Value types in Swift are types that hold their data directly—they are copied when assigned or passed to a function. The primary value types in Swift include:

Integers: Represent whole numbers. Swift provides several integer types, such as `Int` (which is platform-dependent), `UInt` (unsigned integers), `Int8`, `Int16`, `Int32`, and `Int64`.

```swift
let age: Int = 30
```

Floating-Point Numbers: These represent numbers with fractional components. Swift provides two primary types: `Float` (single-precision) and `Double` (double-precision).

```swift
let temperature: Double = 36.6
```

Booleans: Represent true/false values using the `Bool` type.

```swift
let isSwiftAwesome: Bool = true
```

Strings: Represent collections of characters. Swift's `String` type is Unicode-compliant, making it a versatile

49

choice for text manipulation.

```swift
let greeting: String = "Hello, Swift!"
```

Arrays: An ordered collection of values. You can define arrays to hold values of a particular type.

```swift
let fruits: [String] = ["Apple", "Banana", "Cherry"]
```

Dictionaries: A collection of key-value pairs, where each key is unique.

```swift
let person: [String: String] = ["name": "John", "age": "30"]
```

Reference Types

Reference types, on the other hand, hold a reference to the data rather than the data itself. The main reference type in Swift is `Class`. Unlike value types, reference types are not copied when assigned or passed to a function.

```swift
class Car {
var model: String init(model: String) {
self.model = model
}
}

let myCar = Car(model: "Tesla")
let anotherCar = myCar // anotherCar references the same instance as myCar
```

Type Inference

Swift is equipped with a powerful type inference system, allowing the compiler to deduce the data type of a variable based on its initial value. This makes the code cleaner and more concise while maintaining type safety.

```swift
let number = 42 // inferred as Int let pi = 3.14 // inferred as Double
```

Operators in Swift

Operators are special symbols that perform operations on one, two, or three operands. Swift provides various categories of operators that you can use in your code:

Arithmetic Operators

These operators are used for basic mathematical operations, such as addition, subtraction, multiplication, anddivision.

Addition: `+`
Subtraction: `-`
Multiplication: `*`
Division: `/`
Modulo: `%`

```swift
let sum = 5 + 3      // 8
let product = 5 * 3   // 15
let division = 15 / 3 // 5
let remainder = 10 % 3  // 1
```

Compound Assignment Operators

These operators combine assignment with an arithmetic operation.

```swift
```

```
var value = 10
value += 5           // Equivalent to value = value + 5
value -= 3     // Equivalent to value = value - 3
```

Comparison Operators

Comparison operators are used to compare two values. They return a Boolean value indicating whether the comparison is true or false.

Equal to: `==`
Not equal to: `!=`
Greater than: `>`
Less than: `<`
Greater than or equal to: `>=`
Less than or equal to: `<=`

```swift
let isEqual = (5 == 5)            // truelet isGreater = (5 > 3)   // true
```

Logical Operators

Logical operators are used to combine multiple Boolean expressions.

Logical AND: `&&`
Logical OR: `||`
Logical NOT: `!`

```swift
```

```swift
let a = true let b = false
let result = a && b    // false
```

Ternary Conditional Operator

The ternary operator is a shorthand way to express conditional logic. It takes three operands and is a concise alternative to an `if-else` statement.

```swift
let condition = true
let result = condition ? "Yes" : "No" // Returns "Yes"
```

Range Operators

Swift also supports range operators to create sequences of values.

Closed range operator (`...`) includes the upper and lower bounds.
Half-open range operator (`..<`) includes the lower bound but excludes the upper bound.

```swift
let closedRange = 1...5 // 1, 2, 3, 4, 5
let halfOpenRange = 1..<5 // 1, 2, 3, 4
```

Understanding data types and operators is fundamental for leveraging the power of Swift in programming. This chapter provided a thorough overview of the various data types you can work with in Swift, including value and reference types. You also learned how operators function, enabling you to perform a myriad of operations on these data types.

Chapter 4: Control Flow

Learning to properly utilize control flow constructs is essential for creating robust and efficient programs. In Swift, control flow allows you to make decisions, loop through collections, and handle conditions effectively. This chapter will cover various control flow constructs such as conditional statements, looping constructs, and control transfer statements.

4.1 Conditional Statements ### 4.1.1 If Statement
The `if` statement is used to execute a block of code based on the outcome of a condition. If the condition evaluates to true, the code block will run; if not, it will be skipped. Here's a simple example:

```swift
let score = 85

if score >= 90 { print("You have an A!")
} else if score >= 80 { print("You have a B!")
} else if score >= 70 { print("You have a C!")
} else {
print("You need to study harder.")
}
```

In this example, Swift first checks if the score is 90 or higher, and if so, it outputs that you have an A. If not, it checks the other conditions in order until it finds one that is true.

4.1.2 Switch Statement

The `switch` statement allows you to evaluate a value against a list of possible matches. It works similarly to if statements but is often more concise and easier to read, especially when dealing with multiple potential matches. Here's how you might use `switch` in Swift:

```swift
let day = "Tuesday"

switch day { case "Monday":
print("Start of the work week.")case "Tuesday":
print("Second day of the work week.")case "Wednesday":
print("Midweek!")case "Thursday":
print("Almost the weekend.")case "Friday":
print("End of the work week!")
```

```
default:
print("Enjoy your weekend!")
}
```

Each case is checked sequentially until a match is found. If no matches are found, the `default` case handles any unmatched values.

4.1.3 Ternary Conditional Operator

The ternary conditional operator provides a shorthand for writing simple `if-else` statements. Its syntax is:

```swift
condition ? valueIfTrue : valueIfFalse
```

Here's an example:

```swift
let isSunny = true
let weatherMessage = isSunny ? "It's a sunny day!" : "It might rain today."print(weatherMessage)
```

This is a concise way to assign a value based on a condition, helping to keep your code neat.## 4.2 Loops
Loops are constructs that repeat a block of code multiple times until a condition is met or other criteria dictate the termination of the loop. Swift provides several types of loops:

4.2.1 For-In Loop

The `for-in` loop is used to iterate over a sequence, such as arrays, dictionaries, or ranges. Here's how to use it with an array:

```swift
let numbers = [1, 2, 3, 4, 5]

for number in numbers { print("Number: \(number)")
}
```

You can also use a `for-in` loop with a range:

```swift
for index in 1...5 { print("Index: \(index)")
}
```

4.2.2 While Loop

The `while` loop executes a block of code as long as a specified condition is true. It's useful when the number of iterations isn't known beforehand. Here is an example:

```swift
var counter = 5

while counter > 0 { print("Countdown: \(counter)")
counter -= 1
}
```

This loop will print the countdown from 5 to 1.### 4.2.3 Repeat-While Loop
The `repeat-while` loop works similarly to the `while` loop, but it guarantees that the code block will execute at least once before the condition is tested. Here's an example:

```swift
var count = 1

repeat {
print("Count: \(count)")count += 1
} while count <= 5
```

In this case, the loop prints the counts from 1 to 5, starting with 1.## 4.3 Control Transfer Statements
Control transfer statements affect the flow of control within loops and functions. Swift includes several important control transfer statements:

4.3.1 Break

The `break` statement immediately exits a looping structure. Here's how you might use it:

```swift
for number in 1...10 {if number == 5 {
break // Exit the loop when number is 5
}
print(number)
}
```

This loop will print numbers from 1 to 4 and then break out of the loop when the number is 5.### 4.3.2 Continue
The `continue` statement skips the current iteration and proceeds to the next iteration of the loop:

```swift
for number in 1...5 {if number == 3 {
continue // Skip the number 3
}
print(number)
}
```

In this example, the output will be 1, 2, 4, and 5, effectively skipping over the number 3.### 4.3.3 Return
The `return` statement allows you to exit a function and optionally return a value. Here is an example:

```swift
func square(of number: Int) -> Int {return number *
```

```
number
}

let result = square(of: 4)
print("The square of 4 is \(result).")
```

In this function, when `return` is executed, it exits the function and provides the computed result to the caller.

Control flow is a fundamental aspect of programming and is crucial for building logical and efficient software. This chapter introduced you to the various control flow constructs in Swift, including conditional statements, loops, and transfer control statements.

Conditionals in Swift

Conditionals are fundamental constructs in programming that allow us to execute certain pieces of code based on specific conditions. In Swift, conditionals help us control the flow of our programs efficiently. This chapter will explore the different types of conditionals available in Swift, how they work, and practical examples of their use.

1. The `if` Statement

The `if` statement is perhaps the most basic form of conditional logic in Swift. It allows you to execute a block of code if a particular condition evaluates to true.

Syntax

```swift
if condition {
// Code to execute if condition is true
}
```

Example

```swift
let temperature = 30

if temperature > 25 { print("It's a hot day!")
}
```

In this example, the program checks if the temperature is greater than 25. If it is, it prints "It's a hot day!" to the console.

2. The `else` Clause

You can extend an `if` statement with an `else` clause, which will execute if the condition is false.### Syntax
```swift
if condition {
// Code if condition is true
} else {
// Code if condition is false
}
```

Example

```swift
let temperature = 15

if temperature > 25 { print("It's a hot day!")
} else {
print("It's a cool day.")
}
```

In this instance, because the temperature is not greater than 25, the output will be "It's a cool day."## 3. The `else if` Ladder
For situations where you have multiple conditions, you can use `else if` to check additional conditions if the previous ones failed.

Syntax

```swift
if condition1 {
// Code if condition1 is true
} else if condition2 {
// Code if condition2 is true
} else {
// Code if none of the conditions are true
}
```

Example

```swift
let temperature = 0
```

```
if temperature > 25 { print("It's a hot day!")
} else if temperature > 15 {print("It's a warm day.")
} else if temperature > 0 {print("It's a cool day.")
} else {
print("It's freezing!")
}
```

In this example, since the temperature is 0, the output will be "It's freezing!" ## 4. The Ternary Conditional Operator Swift also provides a shorthand way to write conditionals using the ternary conditional operator. It allows for a more compact syntax when assigning values based on a condition.

Syntax

```swift

condition ? valueIfTrue : valueIfFalse
```

Example

```swift
let temperature = 20
let weatherMessage = temperature > 25 ? "It's a hot day!"
: "It's not too hot."print(weatherMessage) // It prints "It's not too hot."
```

In this case, the `weatherMessage` variable will be

assigned "It's not too hot." because the condition is false.
5. Switch Statement
The `switch` statement offers a powerful alternative to `if` statements for checking multiple values. It's particularly useful in handling various conditions based on the same variable.

Syntax

```swift
switch variable {case value1:
// Code for value1case value2:
// Code for value2default:
// Code for all other values
}
```

Example

```swift
let temperature = 10

switch temperature {case 0:
print("It's freezing!")case 1..<15:
print("It's cool.")case 15..<25:
print("It's warm.")case 25...40:
print("It's hot!")default:
print("Temperature is out of range.")
}
```

In this example, since the temperature is 10, the output will be "It's cool."## 6. Using `where` with Switch Cases

Swift allows you to use a `where` clause to add additional conditions to your `switch` cases.### Example
```swift
let temperature = 22

switch temperature { case let x where x < 0:
print("It's freezing!") case let x where x < 15:
print("It's cool.")
case let x where x < 25:print("It's warm.")
case let x where x >= 25:print("It's hot!")
default:
print("Temperature is out of range.")
}
```

Here, the `where` clause is used to make the conditions more flexible, allowing for both value checks and additional logic in the same construct.

Understanding conditionals is vital for controlling the flow of your Swift programs. From simple `if` statements to more complex `switch` cases, Swift provides a variety of tools to handle conditional logic in a readable and efficient way.

Loops in Swift

In Swift, a powerful and modern programming language developed by Apple, loops provide a variety of ways to iterate over sequences such as arrays, dictionaries, and ranges. This chapter explores the different types of loops available in Swift, along with their syntax, use cases, and practical examples.

1. The Basics of Loops

Before diving into the specific loop constructs in Swift, it's essential to understand what loops do. Essentially, a loop will continue to execute a block of code as long as a certain condition is met. In Swift,there are primarily three types of loops:

For-in Loops
While Loops
Repeat-While Loops ### 1.1 For-in Loops
The `for-in` loop is one of the most commonly used loops in Swift. It is particularly useful for iterating over collections like arrays, sets, and dictionaries, as well as ranges of numbers.

Syntax:
```swift
for item in collection {
// Code to execute for each item
}
```

Example:
Suppose you want to print each element of an array:
```swift
let fruits = ["Apple", "Banana", "Cherry"] for fruit in fruits
{
print(fruit)
}
```

```
```

In this example, the loop iterates over each element in the `fruits` array, and the `print` statement outputs each fruit name to the console.

1.1.1 Iterating with Ranges

You can also use `for-in` loops with ranges:
```swift
for number in 1...5 {
print("Current number is \(number)")
}
```

This will print numbers from 1 to 5 inclusive. If you want to exclude the upper bound (5 in this case), you can use half-open ranges:

```swift
for number in 1..<5 {
print("Current number is \(number)")
}
```

This will print numbers from 1 to 4.### 1.2 While Loops
`while` loops are useful when the number of iterations is not predetermined. This loop will continue as long as the specified condition evaluates to true.

Syntax:
```swift
while condition {
// Code to execute as long as the condition is true
```

```
}
```

Example:
```swift
var counter = 0 while counter < 5 {
print("Counter is \(counter)")counter += 1
}
```

In this example, the loop will print the value of the counter until it reaches 5. Note that it's crucial to modify the condition variable within the loop to avoid infinite loops.

1.3 Repeat-While Loops

The `repeat-while` loop is similar to the `while` loop, but the key difference is that the code block will execute at least once before the condition is checked. This can be useful when you need to ensure that the code runs before the condition is tested.

Syntax:
```swift
repeat {
// Code to execute
} while condition
```

Example:
```swift
var index = 0repeat {
print("Index is \(index)")index += 1
```

70

```
} while index < 5
```

In this example, the index will print from 0 to 4 just like the previous loop types, but it guarantees that the print statement runs at least once.

2. Loop Control Statements

Swift provides several control statements that can change the flow of loops:### 2.1 Break Statement
The `break` statement can be used to exit a loop entirely:
```swift
for i in 1...10 {if i == 5 { break
}
print(i)
}
```

This loop will print numbers 1 through 4, as the loop terminates once `i` equals 5.### 2.2 Continue Statement
The `continue` statement skips the current iteration and proceeds to the next one:
```swift
for i in 1...10 { if i % 2 == 0 {
continue
}
print(i)
}
```

This will print odd numbers from 1 to 10, skipping even numbers.### 2.3 Labeled Statements
You can also give names to your loops and use labels with `break` and `continue` to control the flow of nested loops:

```swift
outerLoop: for i in 1...3 {for j in 1...3 {
if i == 2 && j == 2 {break outerLoop
}
print("i: \(i), j: \(j)")
}
}
```

In this case, the output will stop processing when both `i` and `j` are 2.

In this chapter, we have explored the various types of loops in Swift and how they can be effectively used to perform repetitive tasks. The `for-in`, `while`, and `repeat-while` loops provide flexibility to handle different scenarios, while control statements allow fine-tuned management of loop execution. Mastering loops is essential for writing efficient and readable code, making them a core element of programming in Swift. As you continue learning Swift, try integrating loops into your projects to automate tasks and create dynamic applications.

Chapter 5: Functions and Closures in Swift

This chapter will delve into the intricacies of functions and closures in Swift, highlighting their syntax, uses, and the way they enhance the flexibility and functionality of your code.

5.1 Understanding Functions ### 5.1.1 Definition and Syntax
In Swift, a function is a self-contained block of code that performs a specific task. Functions can take inputs, known as parameters, and can return a value. The basic syntax of a function in Swift is as follows:

```swift
func functionName(parameterName: ParameterType) ->
ReturnType {
// Function body
}
```

Example:

```swift
func addNumbers(a: Int, b: Int) -> Int {return a + b
}
```

In the example above, `addNumbers` is a function that takes two parameters of type `Int` and returns their sum as an `Int`.

5.1.2 Calling Functions

To use a function, you simply call it by its name and pass the required arguments. Here's how you can call the `addNumbers` function:

```swift
let sum = addNumbers(a: 5, b: 10)print(sum) // Output: 15
```

5.1.3 Function Parameters and Return Values

Functions can have multiple parameters and can also return different types. Swift provides a way to define parameters as in-out parameters, which allow them to be modified directly.

Example of In-Out Parameters:

```swift
```

```
func swapValues(a: inout Int, b: inout Int) {let temp = a
a = b
b = temp
```

```
}
```

```swift
var x = 10var y = 20
swapValues(&x, &y)
print("x: \(x), y: \(y)") // Output: x: 20, y: 10
```

5.1.4 Default Parameter Values

Swift also allows functions to have default parameter values, making them flexible during function calls.####
Example:
```swift
func greet(name: String, greeting: String = "Hello") {
print("\(greeting), \(name)!")
}
```

```swift
greet(name: "Alice")        // Output: Hello, Alice!
greet(name: "Bob", greeting: "Hi") // Output: Hi, Bob!
```

5.1.5 Variadic Parameters

Sometimes you may want to accept a variable number of parameters. Swift's variadic parameters provide a convenient way to manage this.

Example:

```swift
func sumOfNumbers(numbers: Int...) -> Int { return
numbers.reduce(0, +)
}
```

```
print(sumOfNumbers(numbers: 1, 2, 3, 4)) // Output: 10
```

5.2 Closures: The Anonymous Functions

Closures in Swift are self-contained blocks of functionality
that can be passed around and used in your code. They are
similar to functions but can capture and store references
to variables and constants from the context in which they
are defined.

5.2.1 Syntax and Basic Example

The basic syntax of a closure looks like this:

```swift
{ (parameters) -> ReturnType in
// Closure body
}
```

Example:

```swift
let multiplyClosure = { (a: Int, b: Int) -> Int in return a * b
}

let result = multiplyClosure(3, 4) print(result) // Output:
12
```

5.2.2 Closures as Function Parameters

Closures can be used as parameters for functions, enhancing their flexibility.#### Example:
```swift
func performOperation(operation: (Int, Int) -> Int, a: Int, b: Int) -> Int {return operation(a, b)
}

let operationResult = performOperation(operation: multiplyClosure, a: 5, b: 6) print(operationResult) // Output: 30
```

5.2.3 Trailing Closures

If a closure is the last parameter of a function, you can use a trailing closure syntax for better readability. #### Example:
```swift
func execute(operation: (Int, Int) -> Int, a: Int, b: Int, completion: () -> Void) {let result = operation(a, b)
print("Result: \(result)")completion()
}

execute(operation: { $0 + $1 }, a: 10, b: 5) {
print("Operation completed.")
}
```

5.2.4 Capturing Values

Closures capture and store references to any constants and variables from the surrounding context. This feature is

78

particularly useful for asynchronous programming.

Example:

```swift
func makeIncrementer(incrementAmount: Int) -> () ->
Int {var total = 0
let incrementer: () -> Int = { total += incrementAmount
return total
}
return incrementer
}

let                   incrementByTwo               =
makeIncrementer(incrementAmount: 2)

print(incrementByTwo())        //        Output:        2
print(incrementByTwo()) // Output: 4
```

Functions and closures are pivotal to writing clean and efficient Swift code. They enhance your capabilities to modularize, pass around behavior, and capture state. In this chapter, you learned about defining and using functions, handling parameters and return values, utilizing closures as first-class citizens, and leveraging advanced closure concepts such as capturing values and trailing closures.

Defining and Calling Functions

They are essential for organizing code, reducing

redundancy, and increasing readability. In this chapter, we will explore how to define and call functions in Swift, covering parameters, return types, and different ways to define functions.

What is a Function?

A function is a self-contained block of code that performs a specific task. Functions take inputs, process them, and then produce outputs. In Swift, defining a function involves specifying its name, parameters, and the code required to perform the task. Once defined, you can call the function whenever needed, making your code cleaner and more efficient.

Defining a Function

To define a function in Swift, you use the `func` keyword, followed by the function name and parentheses. Inside the parentheses, you can define parameters. Here's the basic syntax for defining a function:

```swift
func functionName(parameterName: ParameterType) ->
ReturnType {
// Function body
}
```

Example 1: A Simple Function

Let's define a simple function that takes two integers as parameters and returns their sum:

```swift
func addTwoNumbers(a: Int, b: Int) -> Int {return a + b
}
```

In this function, `addTwoNumbers` is the name of the function, `a` and `b` are the parameters of type `Int`, and the function returns an `Int` value, which is their sum.

Example 2: Calling a Function

To call the function we just defined, simply use its name followed by parentheses containing the arguments:

```swift
let sum = addTwoNumbers(a: 5, b: 10)print("The sum is \(sum)")
```

When this code is executed, it prints: "The sum is 15".## Parameters and Return Types
Multiple Parameters

Functions can take multiple parameters by separating them with commas. For example:

```swift
func multiplyThreeNumbers(x: Int, y: Int, z: Int) -> Int {
return x * y * z
}
```

You can call this function similarly:

```swift
let product = multiplyThreeNumbers(x: 2, y: 3, z: 4)
print("The product is \(product)") // Output: The product
is 24
```

Parameter Labels

Swift allows you to specify external parameter names for better readability. These names are included when you call the function but not when you use them inside the function body.

```swift
func divide(numerator: Double, denominator: Double) ->
Double {return numerator / denominator
}
```

When calling the function, you use both parameter names:

```swift
let result = divide(numerator: 10.0, denominator: 2.0)
print("The result is \(result)") // Output: The result is 5.0
```

Default Parameter Values

You can also provide default values for parameters. If the caller does not provide a value, the default value is used:

```swift
func greet(name: String, greeting: String = "Hello") {
print("\(greeting), \(name)!")
}
```

You can call this function with or without the second parameter:

```swift
greet(name: "Alice") // Output: Hello, Alice!
greet(name: "Bob", greeting: "Good Morning") // Output:
Good Morning, Bob!
```

Variadic Parameters

If you want to accept a variable number of arguments, you can use variadic parameters. A parameter marked with `...` takes zero or more values of the specified type.

```swift
func sumOfNumbers(numbers: Int...) -> Int { return
numbers.reduce(0, +)
}
```

You can call this function with any number of integer arguments:

```swift
let total = sumOfNumbers(numbers: 1, 2, 3, 4, 5)
print("The total is \(total)") // Output: The total is 15
```

```
```

Returning Multiple Values

Swift allows functions to return multiple values using tuples. Here's an example:

```swift
func calculateDimensions(length: Double, width: Double)
-> (area: Double, perimeter: Double) {let area = length *
width
let perimeter = 2 * (length + width) return (area,
perimeter)
}
```

You can call this function and access the returned values:

```swift
let dimensions = calculateDimensions(length: 5.0, width:
3.0)
print("Area:        \(dimensions.area),        Perimeter:
\(dimensions.perimeter)")  //  Output:  Area:  15.0,
Perimeter: 16.0
```

Functions are vital for structuring your code and enhancing its readability and maintainability. In the chapters to come, we will delve deeper into more advanced concepts and functional programming paradigms within Swift. Happy coding!

Introduction to Closures

Closures provide a powerful way to encapsulate functionality, enabling developers to write more succinct, reusable, and expressive code. This chapter introduces you to the concept of closures in Swift, exploring their syntax, use cases, and how they can enhance your programming toolkit.

What are Closures?

At its core, a closure is a self-contained block of functionality that can be passed around and used in your code. In simpler terms, closures in Swift are similar to blocks in Objective-C or lambdas in other programming languages such as Java or JavaScript. They can capture and store references to variables and constants from the surrounding context in which they are defined, creating a powerful mechanism for data encapsulation.

Closures can take parameters and return values, making them extremely versatile. They are often used as callback functions, for example, to handle asynchronous operations, manage event responses, or customize a function's behavior.

Closure Syntax

The syntax for closures in Swift can vary depending on how they are defined. Here are the three main forms:

Global Functions: These are closures that have a

85

name and do not capture any values. They can bedefined using the `func` keyword.

```swift
func addNumbers(a: Int, b: Int) -> Int {return a + b
}
```

Nested Functions: These are closures defined within a function and can capture the values ofvariables from the enclosing function's scope.

```swift
func makeIncrementer(incrementAmount: Int) -> () ->
Int {var total = 0
func incrementer() -> Int { total += incrementAmount
return total
}
return incrementer
}
```

Closure Expressions: These are unnamed closures that can be written in a lightweight syntax. Closure expressions can be passed as parameters to functions or stored in variables.

```swift
let add: (Int, Int) -> Int = { (a: Int, b: Int) inreturn a + b

}
```

Capturing Values

One of the most powerful features of closures is their ability to capture and store references to variables and constants from their surrounding context. This means that the closure can use these captured values even after they have gone out of scope. Here's an example:

```swift
func makeIncrementer(incrementAmount: Int) -> () ->
Int {var total = 0
let incrementer: () -> Int = { total += incrementAmount
return total
}
return incrementer
}

let                incrementByTwo          =
makeIncrementer(incrementAmount:           2)
print(incrementByTwo()) // Prints 2
print(incrementByTwo()) // Prints 4
```

In this example, the `incrementer` closure captures the `total` variable and `incrementAmount` constant, allowing it to maintain state between calls, which showcases how closures can form closures around their environment.

Trailing Closure Syntax

Swift also introduces a more readable syntax when the closure is the last argument of a function call. This is known as trailing closure syntax, and it can make your code much cleaner. Here's an example:

```swift
func performOperation(withClosure closure: () -> Void) {
// Some codeclosure()
}

performOperation {
print("This is a trailing closure example!")
}
```

Use Cases of Closures

Closures are prevalent in many aspects of Swift programming:

Asynchronous Operations: Closures are often used as callbacks for handling the results ofasynchronous tasks, such as network requests and animations.

```swift
func fetchData(completion: @escaping (Data?, Error?) -> Void) {
// Simulate an network operation

DispatchQueue.global().async {
// Simulate data let data = Data()
completion(data, nil)
}
}
```

```
fetchData { data, error in
// Handle the fetched data
}
```

Functional Programming Constructs: Swift makes heavy use of closures in its collection methods, such as `map`, `filter`, and `reduce`.

```swift
let numbers = [1, 2, 3, 4, 5]
let squaredNumbers = numbers.map { $0 * $0 }
```

Event Handlers and Delegation: Closures allow for clean and concise representations of event handlers, especially UI-related code in iOS development.

Understanding closures is crucial for mastering Swift programming. They provide a flexible and powerful way to manage functionality and data flow in your applications. From simple tasks to complex asynchronous operations, closures can significantly enhance the readability and maintainability of your code.

Chapter 6: Object-Oriented Programming

Swift, Apple's powerful and intuitive programming language, fully embraces OOP principles, allowing developers to build modular and reusable code. In this chapter, we'll explore the fundamental concepts of OOP in Swift, including classes, objects, inheritance, polymorphism, and encapsulation.

6.1 Understanding Classes and Objects ### 6.1.1 Classes
In Swift, a class is a blueprint for creating objects (instances). It defines properties (data) and methods (functions) that the objects will have. Classes enable you to encapsulate related functionalities in a single package, making your code cleaner and more manageable.

Here's a simple class definition in Swift:

```swift
swift class Dog {
// Properties
var name: Stringvar breed: Stringvar age: Int

// Initializer
init(name: String, breed: String, age: Int) { self.name = name
self.breed = breedself.age = age
}

// Method funcbark() {
print("\(name) says Woof!")
```

```
}
}
```

In this example, the `Dog` class has three properties:
`name`, `breed`, and `age`, along with an initializer that
sets the property values when a `Dog` object is created.
The `bark` method is a behavior associated with the
`Dog` class.

6.1.2 Creating Objects

Once you have defined a class, you can create objects from
it. Here's how you can create a `Dog` object:

```swift
let myDog = Dog(name: "Buddy", breed: "Golden
Retriever", age: 3) myDog.bark() // Output: Buddy says
Woof!
```

In this example, `myDog` is an instance of the `Dog` class. The properties `name`, `breed`, and `age` are set through the initializer, and the `bark` method is called to demonstrate behavior.

6.2 Inheritance

Inheritance allows a class to inherit properties and methods from another class. This mechanism promotes code reuse and establishes a hierarchical relationship between classes.

6.2.1 Creating a Subclass

To create a subclass in Swift, you use the colon (`:`) syntax to specify the superclass. Here's an example:

```swift
class Puppy: Dog { var isPlayful: Bool

init(name: String, breed: String, age: Int, isPlayful: Bool) {
self.isPlayful = isPlayful
super.init(name: name, breed: breed, age: age)
}

override func bark() { print("\(name) says Yip Yip!")
}
}
```

In this example, `Puppy` is a subclass of `Dog`. It inherits the properties and methods of the `Dog` class but introduces an additional property `isPlayful` and overrides the `bark` method to provide a different implementation.

6.2.2 Using Subclasses

You can create a `Puppy` object just as you would with a `Dog` object:

```swift
let myPuppy = Puppy(name: "Bella", breed: "Beagle", age: 1, isPlayful: true) myPuppy.bark() // Output: Bella says Yip Yip!
```

This usage demonstrates the principles of inheritance, enabling the `Puppy` class to utilize the functionality of the `Dog` class while extending or modifying it.

6.3 Polymorphism

Polymorphism is the ability to treat objects of different classes through a common interface. This concept allows for flexibility and the ability to interchange objects dynamically.

6.3.1 Method Overriding

As shown in the previous example, subclasses can override methods from their superclass. This is a form of polymorphism, where the behavior of a method can vary based on the object's actual class. For instance:

```swift
```

```
let myDogs: [Dog] = [myDog, myPuppy] for dog in
myDogs {
dog.bark() // Output: Buddy says Woof! \n Bella says Yip
Yip!
}
```

Here, a collection of `Dog` references is created, but it
contains both `Dog` and `Puppy` objects. The appropriate
`bark` method is invoked based on the actual object type.

6.4 Encapsulation

Encapsulation is a key concept in OOP that restricts
access to certain components of an object and only exposes
what is necessary. This is achieved through access control
modifiers.

6.4.1 Access Control

Swift provides several access control levels:

Public: Accessible from any file and module.
Internal: Accessible within the same module (default
access level).
Fileprivate: Accessible within the same source file.
Private: Accessible only within the enclosing
declaration. Example:
```swift
class Cat {
private var name: String

init(name: String) { self.name = name
}
```

```
func getName() -> String {return name
}
}
```
` ` `

In this case, the property `name` is private, meaning it cannot be accessed directly from outside the `Cat` class. It can only be accessed through the public method `getName`.

Object-Oriented Programming in Swift provides a powerful framework for organizing and managing code through classes and objects. By utilizing principles such as inheritance, polymorphism, and encapsulation, developers can create scalable, maintainable, and reusable code structures. As you continue to explore Swift, these OOP fundamentals will be crucial for building robust applications and understanding advanced programming concepts.

Classes and Structures

These two fundamental building blocks allow developers to model complex data and behaviors elegantly. In this chapter, we will explore the syntax and functionality of classes and structures in Swift, compare their characteristics, and discuss when to use each.

What Are Classes and Structures?

Both classes and structures are used to create custom data types that can encapsulate properties and behavior. They allow developers to define complex data models in a way

that is both organized and easy to manage.
However, they have some key differences that affect how they are used in practice.### Classes
A class in Swift is a reference type, which means that when you create an instance of a class and assign it to a variable, you are actually referring to the same instance of that class. That means that if you change the instance using one variable, the change will be reflected in all references to that instance. Classes can also support inheritance, allowing one class to inherit properties and methods from another.

Here's a simple example of a class in Swift:

```swift
class Car {
// Properties
var make: String var model: Stringvar year: Int

// Initializer
init(make: String, model: String, year: Int) {self.make = make
self.model = modelself.year = year
}

// Method
func displayCarInfo() { print("\(year) \(make) \(model)")
}
}

// Usage
let car1 = Car(make: "Toyota", model: "Corolla", year: 2021) car1.displayCarInfo() // Output: 2021 Toyota Corolla
```

```
let car2 = car1 // car2 is a reference to car1 car2.year =
2022
car1.displayCarInfo() // Output: 2022 Toyota Corolla
```

Structures

Structures in Swift are value types, meaning that when you create an instance of a structure and assign it to a variable, you are copying the instance, not referencing it. Changes made to one instance will not affect another. This distinction is pivotal in many programming scenarios, particularly those that require immutability.

Here's an example of a structure in Swift:

```swift
struct Bicycle {
// Properties
var make: String var model: Stringvar year: Int

// Method
func displayBicycleInfo() { print("\(year) \(make) \(model)")
}
}

// Usage
var bicycle1 = Bicycle(make: "Giant", model: "Defy", year: 2020)bicycle1.displayBicycleInfo() // Output: 2020 Giant Defy

var bicycle2 = bicycle1 // bicycle2 is a copy of bicycle1
bicycle2.year = 2021
bicycle1.displayBicycleInfo() // Output: 2020 Giant Defy
```

Key Differences Between Classes and Structures

Understanding the differences between classes and

structures is crucial for writing efficient and clean Swift code. Below are the primary distinctions:

Reference vs. Value Type:
- Classes are reference types; structures are value types. This means classes share a single instance whilestructures create a new copy for each assignment.

Inheritance:
- Classes can inherit from other classes, enabling a hierarchy of functionality. Structures do not support inheritance.

Deinitializers:
- Classes can have deinitializers, which allow you to run cleanup code before the instance is deallocated.Structures do not have deinitializers.

Identity:
- Classes can be compared by identity (using the identity operator `===`), whereas structures are compared by value (i.e., their contents).

Mutability:
- Value types (structures) are immutable when assigned to a constant variable. Reference types (classes), onthe other hand, can be mutated regardless of the variable being a constant.

When to Use Classes and When to Use Structures

The decision to use classes or structures often depends on the specific requirements of your application. Here are some guidelines to aid in your decision-making process:

Use Classes When:

Inheritance: You need to create a base class that can be extended by other classes.
Identity: You want to create an object that should be referenced and shared across multiple places in your application.
Complexity: Your data model requires some form of shared state that should influence multiple parts of your application.

Use Structures When:

Simplicity: The data model is simple and represents values (e.g., coordinates, size, or range).
Immutability: You want to ensure that your data cannot be modified after it's created, promoting safer code.
Performance: Structures can be more efficient in certain scenarios due to their value-type nature, especially when working with small, lightweight objects.

Classes and structures are integral components of Swift, each enchanting with their distinct characteristics and capabilities. Understanding the differences between them allows developers to make informed decisions about which one to use when designing their data models. Whether you are building a simple application or a complex system, mastering classes and structures will empower you to leverage Swift's full potential.

Inheritance and Polymorphism

In Swift, these principles not only enable developers to build complex data models but also empower them to establish relationships between different classes. This chapter delves into the intricacies of inheritance and polymorphism within the Swift programming language, illustrating how these concepts can be harnessed effectively.

Understanding Inheritance

Inheritance is a mechanism wherein a new class, known as a subclass, derives attributes and behaviors (methods) from an existing class, known as a superclass. This establishes an "is-a" relationship—where thesubclass is a specialized version of the superclass.

Basic Syntax of Inheritance

To create a subclass in Swift, you use a colon (:) followed by the superclass's name. Here's a simple example to illustrate this:

```swift
class Animal { var name: String

init(name: String) { self.name = name
}
```

102

```
func makeSound() { print("\(name) makes a sound.")
}
}

class Dog: Animal {
override func makeSound() {print("\(name) barks.")
}
}
```

In this example, `Dog` is a subclass of `Animal`. It inherits the property `name` and the initializer from `Animal`, and it overrides the `makeSound()` method to provide specific behavior for dogs. ### The 'override' Keyword
When a subclass wants to modify a method or property inherited from its superclass, it uses the `override` keyword. This is crucial to ensure that the programmer is aware that they are changing inherited behavior,thereby maintaining clear and manageable code.

Properties and Methods

In Swift, subclasses inherit both properties and methods from their superclasses. They can also define new properties and methods specific to themselves. The following example demonstrates this:

```swift
class Cat: Animal {var color: String

init(name: String, color: String) {self.color = color
```
103

```
    super.init(name: name) // Call to the superclass's
    initializer
    }

    override func makeSound() { print("\(name), the \(color)
    cat, meows.")
    }
}
```

In this case, `Cat` introduces a new property `color` while still extending the `Animal` class.## Polymorphism Polymorphism is the ability of different classes to be treated as instances of the same class through a common interface. In Swift, polymorphism typically manifests through method overriding, enabling a single method to behave differently based on the object that it is invoked on.

Using Base Class References

Consider the following example, where we work with different subclasses of the `Animal` class:

```swift
let animals: [Animal] = [Dog(name: "Rex"), Cat(name: "Whiskers", color: "black")]

for animal in animals {
animal.makeSound() // Polymorphic behavior
}
```

Here, we can create an array of `Animal` type while holding both `Dog` and `Cat` instances. When we call `makeSound()`, the appropriate subclass's implementation is executed, demonstrating polymorphism. This allows the use of a unified interface while preserving unique behaviors.

Dynamic Type Checking

Swift also allows for dynamic type checking to determine the actual class of an object at runtime. This can be performed using the `is` and `as` operators:

```swift
for animal in animals {
if let dog = animal as? Dog { print("\(dog.name) is a dog.")
} else if let cat = animal as? Cat {print("\(cat.name) is a cat.")
}
}
```

In this example, we check the type of each `animal` and cast it accordingly to execute type-specific operations.

Inheritance and polymorphism in Swift provide powerful tools for building flexible, maintainable, and efficient applications. By leveraging inheritance, developers can create rich hierarchies of classes that promote code reusability. Polymorphism further enables these hierarchies to work seamlessly together, allowing functions to operate on shared interfaces with distinct implementations.

Chapter 7: Building Your First App - Idea to Design

Building an app can be an incredibly fulfilling experience, as it allows you to express your creativity and solve real-world problems. By the end of this chapter, you will have a solid understanding of the key concepts in app design and development, and you'll be well on your way to launching your first application.

Step 1: Ideation

Every great app starts with a brilliant idea. Before you start coding, it's crucial to take a step back and think about what you want to create. Here are some steps to help you refine your idea:

Identify a Problem: Successful apps often solve a particular problem or fulfill a specific need. Consider what issues you or those around you face regularly. For instance, is there a task that seems overly complicated?

Research the Market: Look for existing apps that might be similar to your idea. Analyze their strengths and weaknesses. This research will help you understand if your idea is unique or how you can improve upon what is already available.

Define Your Audience: Determine who your target users are. Knowing your audience will guide many aspects of your design and functionality. Are they teenagers, busy professionals, or seniors?

Create User Personas: Develop user personas based on your target audience. This practice involves creating fictional representations of your ideal users, allowing you to tailor your app's features to better meet their needs.

Step 2: Defining Core Features

Now that you have a clear idea of what you want to build and for whom, it's time to outline the core features of your app. Focus on the fundamental functionalities that will provide value to your users:

Prioritize Features: List all the features you would like your app to have, then categorize them into 'must-have' and 'nice-to-have' features. Start by designing the core functionalities because they will form the foundation of your app.

Create a User Journey: Draft user stories that explain how your users will interact with your app. What steps will they take to achieve their goals? This exercise will help you visualize the user experience (UX).

Step 3: Sketching Your App

Before diving into Swift development, it's essential to put your ideas on paper—literally! Sketching helps you visualize the layout and navigation of your app:

Wireframing: Create wireframes for each screen of your app. This can be as simple as a paper prototype or digital tools like Balsamiq, Figma, or Adobe XD.

Wireframes represent the skeletal framework of your app and are critical for user flow.

Define the Navigation: Define how users will navigate through the app. Ensure that the flow is logical and intuitive. Consider using standard navigation patterns that users are familiar with, such as tab bars or side menus.

Step 4: Designing the UI

Once you have wireframes, it's time to add aesthetics. Good design can significantly enhance user experience and retention.

Color Scheme and Typography: Choose a color palette that reflects your brand and the emotions you want to evoke in your users. Select complementary fonts that are easy to read both in standard and small sizes.

Mockups: Transform your wireframes into high-fidelity mockups. Use design tools like Sketch or Figma to bring your sketches to life. Focus on designing each element carefully, ensuring that buttons, icons, and other UI components are visually appealing and functional.

User Testing: After creating mockups, gather feedback from potential users. Conduct usability testing to see how they interact with the designs. Their insights can reveal areas of confusion or improvement.

Step 5: Getting Started with Swift

With robust designs in place, it's time to translate your vision into code using Swift:

Setting Up Xcode: Download and set up Xcode, Apple's integrated development environment (IDE) for macOS. Create a new project and select a template that best fits your app type—such as a single-view app or a tabbed application.

Understanding Swift Basics: Familiarize yourself with the Swift programming language. Focus on fundamental programming concepts like variables, functions, and control flows. Apple's documentation and online resources make for excellent starting points.

Using Interface Builder: Use Interface Builder within Xcode to layout your UI visually. Drag and drop elements like labels, buttons, text fields, etc., onto your view controller. Set Constraints to achieve a responsive layout.

Connecting UI to Code: Learn how to connect UI elements to your Swift code using IBOutlets and IBActions. This step is crucial for making your app interactive.

As you move forward, remember that building an app is an iterative process; you'll continually refine your design and features based on user feedback and testing.

Brainstorming App Ideas

The world of app development is both exciting and

challenging. The rise of mobile technology has created immense opportunities for developers to create applications that can solve real-world problems, entertain, educate, or enhance productivity. This chapter will guide you through the brainstorming process for app ideas, specifically focusing on how to implement such ideas using Swift, Apple's powerful and intuitive programming language.

Understanding the Landscape

Before diving right into idea generation, it's essential to understand the mobile app landscape. As of 2024, millions of apps are available across various categories, including productivity, social media, gaming, health, and education. However, this saturation also indicates a growing need for innovative solutions and fresh ideas.

When brainstorming app ideas, consider the following trends:

User-Centric Applications: Apps that focus on user experience and meet specific needs.
AI and Machine Learning: Integrating AI for personalized recommendations or automation.
Health and Wellness: Mental health apps, fitness trackers, and nutritional guides have gained significant popularity.
Sustainability: Apps promoting eco-friendliness and conscious consumerism.
Remote Work Tools: Solutions that enhance productivity in a remote work environment.## Identifying Problems to Solve

The best app ideas often stem from identifying a problem that needs to be solved. Here are some steps to uncover potential areas of opportunity:

Personal Experiences: Reflect on challenges you face daily. Often, the best ideas come from your struggles, whether it's time management, health tracking, or social interactions.

Market Research: Investigate existing apps, read reviews, and look at what users are asking for. What frustrates them about current options? What features are they missing?

Community Engagement: Join forums, social media groups, or attend meetups related to your area of interest. Engaging with potential users can provide valuable insights and uncover needs you hadn't thought of.

Brainstorming Sessions: Gather a group of friends or colleagues and conduct a brainstorming session. Encourage everyone to share their ideas, no matter how wild they may seem. Sometimes, the craziest ideas can lead to something viable.

Generating App Ideas

With a clear understanding of what to look for, it's time to generate actual app ideas. Below are several categories to consider, along with example ideas that leverage Swift's capabilities.

Productivity Apps

Smart Task Manager: An AI-driven app that prioritizes tasks based on deadlines, user habits, and work patterns. Using Swift and Core Data, users can sync tasks across devices seamlessly.

Focus Enhancer: An app that combines Pomodoro techniques with ambient sounds, helping users maintain focus. Swift's AVFoundation makes it easy to integrate sound features.

Health and Fitness Apps

Personal Wellness Coach: An app that provides personalized workout regimes and dietary tips based on user input and progress tracking.

Mindfulness Tracker: A platform that encourages users to practice mindfulness with guided sessions, reminders, and mood tracking, utilizing SwiftUI for a smooth and engaging UI.

Social Networking Apps

Local Connection Hub: An app designed for connecting people who live nearby based on shared interests or activities. Utilizing CloudKit, users can stay connected with ease.

Event Organizer: Something like a mini Facebook for local community events where users can create, discover, and RSVP to events. Swift's networking capabilities can help with real-time updates.

Educational Apps

Interactive Learning Hub: An app that offers bite-sized lessons on various subjects with quizzes and achievements. Swift can be used to create interactive content that's both engaging and educational.

Language Exchange Platform: Pairing language learners from different backgrounds for conversational practice, utilizing Swift's capabilities for voice recognition.

Prototyping Your Idea in Swift

Once you've settled on an app idea or several ideas you'd like to explore, the next step is to create a prototype. This stage is crucial as it allows you to visualize functionality and design.

Sketch Your Idea: Start with low-fidelity wireframes on paper or digital tools like Sketch or Figma. Focus on the flow and usability of your app.

Choose Your Tools: Xcode is the primary tool for developing apps in Swift. Familiarize yourself with its interface and functionalities.

Develop Basic Features: Start coding essential features using Swift. Use SwiftUI for building your user interface, as it allows for quick iterations and previews.

Conduct User Testing: Share your prototype with potential users and gather feedback. Iterate based on their responses to refine both functionality and design.

By understanding the trends, identifying needs, and leveraging tools like Swift, you can not only generate innovative ideas but also bring them to life. Remember that every great app starts with a simple idea, and through experimentation and refinement, it can evolve into something remarkable. Embrace the journey of app development; the opportunities are limitless!

Creating Wireframes and Mockups

Before diving into lines of code, it is crucial to create a tangible representation of your app's user interface and user experience. Wireframes and mockups serve as blueprints that guide the development process and ensure that all stakeholders are aligned with the app's vision. In this chapter, we'll delve into the techniques and tools that can help you create effective wireframes and mockups for your Swift applications.

Understanding Wireframes and Mockups

Wireframes are low-fidelity sketches of an application. They focus on layout, structure, and functionality without getting bogged down by design details. Wireframes serve as a foundation, allowing you to plan the user journey, arrange content hierarchies, and provide a basic visual representation of the app.

Mockups, on the other hand, are high-fidelity representations that incorporate color, typography, images, and other design elements. They showcase the app's design in a more polished way, providing a closer look at how the final product will appear.

In essence, wireframes are functional guides, while mockups are design blueprints. ## Tools for Creating Wireframes and Mockups
There are several tools available for creating wireframes and mockups, each with its own strengths. Here are a few popular options:

Sketch: A powerful vector-based design tool that is popular among UI/UX designers. It's great for creating both wireframes and high-fidelity mockups with support for plugins and collaborative design.

Figma: A cloud-based design tool that allows for real-time collaboration. Figma is excellent for both wireframing and mockups, making it easy for teams to work together from different locations.

Adobe XD: Part of the Adobe Creative Cloud suite, XD provides tools for wireframing and creating interactive prototypes. It integrates well with other Adobe products, making it a good choice for designers already using Adobe tools.

Balsamiq: A dedicated wireframing tool that emphasizes simplicity and speed. It's perfect for creating quick sketches and low-fidelity wireframes without getting distracted by design details.

Axure RP: A robust tool that allows for detailed

wireframes, mockups, and interactive prototypes. It's best for complex applications where user interaction is critical.

Creating Wireframes for Your Swift App ### Step 1: Define User Stories and Use Cases
Before you start wireframing, define the user stories and use cases for your app. Understanding the goals, needs, and pain points of your users will help you prioritize the features and layout of your app. Create a list of essential screens and outline the primary actions users will take in your app.

Step 2: Sketch the Basic Layout

Using your chosen wireframing tool, begin by sketching the basic layout of each screen. Focus on structural elements such as headers, footers, navigation bars, and content areas. Use placeholders for images and text,

and aim to outline how users will navigate through the app. ### Step 3: Create a Flowchart
To visualize user journeys, create flowcharts that illustrate how users will interact with different screens. This exercise helps identify any potential bottlenecks or points of confusion within the user experience. It's also helpful in ensuring that every user story is covered.

Step 4: Iterate and Gather Feedback

Once you have a preliminary wireframe, gather feedback from team members or potential users. This stage is crucial for evaluating usability and functionality before investing too much time in design. Iterate on the wireframe based on the feedback you receive.

Transitioning to Mockups

Once you have a solid wireframe, you will want to transition into creating mockups. This is where you can add attention to detail that enhances the user experience visually.

Step 1: Set Up a Design System

Design consistency is key in mobile development. Establish a design system that includes color palettes, typography, button styles, and spacing guidelines. This system will streamline the mockup process and ensure uniformity throughout your app.

Step 2: Apply Visual Elements

Using your wireframe as a foundation, begin adding visual elements to your design. Use the design system you created to select colors, fonts, and icons that reflect your app's brand identity. Pay attention to hierarchy and spacing to ensure the UI remains intuitive.

Step 3: Create Interactive Mockups

Leveraging tools like Figma or Adobe XD, create interactive mockups that simulate the user experience. This allows stakeholders to click through the app and experience the user interface as if it were a live application. It's an excellent way to showcase transitions and animations.

Step 4: Test and Revise

Share your mockups with users and gather feedback. Usability testing is a crucial step in identifying design flaws and areas for improvement. Keep refining your mockups based on user testing results to ensure an optimal user experience.

Integrating Wireframes and Mockups with Swift Development

Once your wireframes and mockups are finalized, you can begin translating these designs into Swift code. Use Interface Builder in Xcode to create layouts that match your mockups closely.

Step 1: Storyboards and SwiftUI

Choose between using storyboards and UIKit or adopting SwiftUI for a more modern approach. SwiftUI allows you to create declarative interfaces that can dynamically respond to changes in data and state.

Step 2: Component Reusability

Leverage component reusability in your Swift code to ensure that your UI remains consistent. Create custom views that encapsulate specific functionalities or UI elements, making it easier to maintain and update your codebase.

Step 3: Implementing Design Guidelines

119

Follow Apple's Human Interface Guidelines to ensure your app meets platform standards and provides a familiar experience for users. This includes maintaining accessibility, responsiveness, and clarity in your designs.

With the right tools and techniques, you can build an app that not only meets the needs of your users but also creates a seamless and engaging experience. In the rapidly evolving world of mobile development, investing time in planning and design is the key to delivering a product that stands out in the Marketplace.

Chapter 8: Building Your First App - Setting Upthe Project

In this chapter, we will take our first steps into the exciting world of iOS app development by creating a simple application using Swift and Xcode. Setting up a project correctly is crucial for ensuring a smooth development process, so we'll explore the necessary steps from installing Xcode to configuring your project settings.

8.1 Installing Xcode

Before we dive into project configuration, the first thing we need to do is install Xcode, the official Integrated Development Environment (IDE) for iOS app development. Follow these steps to get started:

Download Xcode:
Open the Mac App Store.
Search for "Xcode".
Click the "Get" or "Download" button and install it.

Open Xcode:
Once installed, locate Xcode in your Applications folder or launch it from Spotlight by pressing
`Command () + Space` and typing "Xcode".
When you open Xcode for the first time, you might be prompted to install additional components. Allow it to proceed as these are necessary for development.

Check for Updates:

- Keeping Xcode updated ensures you have the latest features and bug fixes. Navigate to Xcode >Preferences > Components to manage your updates.

8.2 Creating a New Project

Open Xcode and start a new project:
- Click "Create a new Xcode project" on the welcome screen or go to `File > New > Project`.

Select a Template:
- You'll be presented with a variety of templates for your project. For our basic app, choose the "App" template under the iOS tab. This provides a solid foundation for an iOS application.

Configure Your Project:
Product Name: Enter the name of your app. This is how it will be displayed to users.
Team: If you have an Apple Developer account, select your team. If not, you can leave it as "None" for now.
Organization Identifier: This is typically a reverse domain name (e.g., `com.yourname`).
Interface: Choose "Storyboard" if you prefer a visual approach to designing your UI. If you feel adventurous, you can opt for "SwiftUI".
Language: Ensure "Swift" is selected.
Use Core Data and Include Tests: For this simple app, leave these unchecked. We can explore these advanced concepts later.

Choose a Location:
- Choose a directory on your computer where you would

like to save your project. This is where all your project files will reside.

Create:
- Click "Create," and Xcode will generate your project files and open the main workspace.## 8.3 Understanding the Xcode Interface
Upon creating the project, take a moment to familiarize yourself with the Xcode interface:

Navigator Area: Located on the left side, it provides access to your files, build settings, and documentation.
Editor Area: In the center, this is where you'll interact with your code or design your UI.
Utility Area: To the right, it contains inspectors for various attributes of selected elements (like properties of a UIView) and a library containing UI components.
Toolbar: At the top, the toolbar gives you control to run your app, manage schemes, and debug.## 8.4 Setting Project Targets and Deployment Info
Before running your app, let's configure some essential settings:

Select the Project in the Navigator:
- Click on the top level of your project (the one with your Product Name) in the Navigator to access the project settings.

General Tab:
- Under the "Deployment Info" section, ensure that you set the correct target iOS version. This determines what versions of iOS your app will support.

Device Orientation:
- Choose the device orientations that your app will support (Portrait, Landscape Left, etc.).

Versioning:
- Update your version number and build number if necessary. This is especially important for app updates in the App Store.

Target Devices:
- Specify whether your app is for iPhone, iPad, or both by selecting the appropriate options under "Devices".

8.5 Building and Running Your Project

Now that we've set up the project, let's launch our first app:

Choose a Simulator:
- In the toolbar, use the device dropdown to select a simulator (e.g., iPhone 14 Pro).

Build and Run:
- Press the "Run" button (or hit `Command () + R`) to build and run your app. The simulator will launch, and your app will appear.

Debugging:
- If you make any mistakes, Xcode's console will provide error messages to help you debug. Familiarize yourself with reading these logs; they will become invaluable throughout development.

Congratulations! You have successfully set up your first iOS app project in Swift. You've installed Xcode, created a new app, configured basic settings, and learned how to run your application in a simulated environment. As we progress through the upcoming chapters, you will gain deeper insights into how to build your app's user interface and implement functionality.

Creating a New Project in Xcode

In this chapter, we will walk through the process of creating a new project in Xcode using Swift, Apple's powerful and intuitive programming language for iOS, macOS, watchOS, and tvOS development. Xcode is the official integrated development environment (IDE) for Apple's platforms, and it provides a comprehensive suite of tools to help developers create high-quality applications.

Getting Started

Before we can dive into creating our new project, you'll need to ensure that you have Xcode installed on your macOS system. You can download it for free from the Mac App Store. Once you've installed Xcode, you can launch the application and begin the setup process for your new project.

Step 1: Launching Xcode

Open Xcode: Start by locating the Xcode app in your Applications folder or through Spotlight search.

Welcome Window: Upon launching, you will be greeted with the welcome window, which provides options to start a new project, open an existing project, or access recent files.

Step 2: Creating a New Project

Select "Create a new Xcode project": Click on the "Create a new Xcode project" option in the welcome window. If the welcome window does not appear, you can select "File" from the menu bar, then choose "New," followed by "Project."

Choose a Template: The next screen presents various templates for your new project. Choose an appropriate platform—iOS, macOS, watchOS, or tvOS. For this chapter, we will select **iOS** and then choose the **App** template. This template is suitable for general application development.

Click "Next": Once you've selected the template, click the "Next" button to proceed to the configuration screen for your new project.

Step 3: Configuring Your Project

On this screen, you will be prompted to provide several important details about your new project:

Product Name: Enter the name of your application. This is how your app will be identified on devices and in the App Store.

127

Team: If you have an Apple Developer account, select your development team from the dropdown. If you don't have one, you can select "None" for now, but later on, you will need a developer account for deploying your app to physical devices.

Organization Name: This is typically your name or your company's name, and it will be used to identify the app's source.

Organization Identifier: This is a reverse domain name style identifier (for example, `com.example`). This identifier, in combination with your product name, uniquely identifies your app.

Interface: Choose the user interface design style:
Storyboard (traditional interface builder) or
SwiftUI (a newer declarative framework). If you're just starting with iOS development, it might be beneficial to choose Storyboard, but feel free to explore SwiftUI if you're interested in the latest frameworks.

Language: Ensure that Swift is selected as the programming language for your application.

Use Core Data: If your application will require data persistence, you can check this box to add Core Data support.

Include Tests: Decide if you want to include unit and UI testing options for your project.

After filling in all required fields, click on the **Next** button.### Step 4: Choosing a Location for Your Project You will now be prompted to choose a location to save your project.

Select Location: Choose a directory where you want your project folder to be stored. It's generally a good practice to create a dedicated folder for your Xcode projects for better organization.

Create Git Repository (Optional): You can also choose to create a Git repository for your project. This can be useful for version control and collaborative development. If you choose to do so, simply check the box that says "Create a Git repository on my Mac."

Click "Create": Once you have selected the location and configured your preferences, click the "Create" button.

Step 5: Exploring the Xcode Interface

Congratulations! You have just created a new Xcode project in Swift. Upon clicking "Create," Xcode will generate your project files and present you with the main Xcode interface, which is divided into several distinct areas:

Navigator Area: Displays the file structure of your project and allows you to navigate between files.
Editor Area: Where you'll write and edit your Swift code, as well as design your UI.
Utilities Area: Contains libraries of project assets, code snippets, and object libraries. You can find UI

components here if you're working with Storyboards.
Debug Area: Displays console output and allows you to debug your application. ### Step 6: Running Your Application
To test your new application, you can run it on a simulator or a physical device:

Select a Simulator: In the toolbar, you will see a dropdown menu for choosing a simulator. Select one of the available options (e.g., iPhone 14).

Build and Run: Click the **Play** button (or use the shortcut Command + R) to build and run your application. Xcode will compile your code and launch the simulator, displaying your blank app interface.

In the following chapters, we will dive deeper into creating user interfaces, managing project files, and implementing functionality in your new app. By mastering these foundational skills, you will be well on your way to developing impressive applications for Apple platforms.

Configuring Project Settings

In this chapter, we will explore how to configure project settings in a Swift environment, particularly within Xcode, Apple's integrated development environment (IDE). Understanding these settings will help streamline your development process and improve application performance and compatibility.

1. Setting Up Your Xcode Project

When you create a new project in Xcode, the first step is to select the appropriate template for your application. Xcode offers various templates, such as Single View App, Tabbed App, and Game, each tailored for specific application types.

1.1. Creating a New Project

Open Xcode and select "Create a new Xcode project."
Choose the appropriate template for your application.
Fill in the project details, including Product Name, Team, Organization Name, and OrganizationIdentifier.
Choose the programming language (Swift) and the user interface style (UIKit, SwiftUI).
Click "Next" and choose a location to save your project. ## 2. Navigating the Project Settings
Once your project is created, you can access the project settings through the project navigator. Click on the project file (usually named after your product) at the top of the left pane.

2.1. Overview of Project Settings

By clicking on the project file, you will see two main sections of settings: **Project** and **Targets**.

Project: Contains settings that apply to the entire project, like the deployment target and build configurations.
Targets: Contains settings specific to each target in your project (e.g., your app, test targets, etc.). ## 3.

131

Configuring Build Settings

The Build Settings tab contains numerous options that control how the project is compiled and linked. Here are some essential settings to consider:

3.1. Deployment Info

In the **General** tab under the target settings, you'll find **Deployment Info**. Here, you can set the minimum iOS version your app supports. By doing this, you ensure that users on older devices can still use your app, while leveraging newer features on supported systems.

3.2. Build Configurations

Xcode typically configures three build configurations: Debug, Release, and Profile. You can modify these according to your project's needs:

Go to the **Build Settings** tab.
Under the **Configurations** section, you can add or remove configurations.

Each configuration allows you to specify different optimization levels or settings for development and production environments.

3.3. Architectures

In the **Build Settings** tab, you'll find the **Architectures** setting which specifies which CPU architectures your app supports. You can manage build architectures (e.g., arm64, x86_64) here, especially if you're working on a cross-platform app or targeting emulators.

4. Configuring Code Signing

Code signing is critical for app distribution, especially when submitting to the App Store. You must configure your code signing settings in Xcode correctly.

4.1. Signing & Capabilities

Select your target, go to the **Signing & Capabilities** tab, and configure the following:

Enable automatic signing if you'd like Xcode to manage your provisioning profiles and certificates.
Choose the appropriate development team.
Ensure that the Bundle Identifier is unique to prevent conflicts with other apps. ### 4.2. App Capabilities
Under the same tab, you can enable capabilities specific to your app:
In-App Purchases
Push Notifications
Background Modes

Activating these capabilities allows you to leverage unique iOS features, making your app more robust. ## 5. Managing Dependencies
For many developers, managing external libraries and frameworks is a critical aspect of project setup. You can use Swift Package Manager, Carthage, or CocoaPods to manage dependencies.

5.1. Swift Package Manager

Swift Package Manager (SPM) is built directly into Xcode. You can add packages through Xcode:

Select your project file.
Go to the **Package Dependencies** section.
Click the "+" button to add a new package dependency.
Enter the repository URL and select the version you want to integrate.## 6. Configuring the Info.plist File
The `Info.plist` file contains essential configuration details about your application, such as:

App display name
Version number
App icons
Permissions (e.g., accessing camera, location services)

Editing the `Info.plist` within Xcode's file navigator allows you to customize these settings easily.

7. Preparing for Release

As your project nears completion, you'll want to validate your configurations and prepare for release.### 7.1. Build for Distribution
Ensure that your app builds correctly in Release configuration. Test all functionalities and perform a thorough QA process before submission.

7.2. Archiving Your App

To submit your app, you will need to create an archive:

Select your target device as "Generic iOS Device."
Go to Product > Archive.
Once the archive is created, navigate to the Organizer window to validate and distribute your app.

Configuring project settings in Swift using Xcode can seem daunting at first, but mastering these settings is essential for successful app development and deployment. This chapter has guided you through creating a project, navigating and configuring different settings, handling dependencies, and preparing your app for release. As you advance in your Swift development journey, these configuration skills will serve as a foundation for building robust and successful applications.

Chapter 9: Designing the User Interface

A well-designed UI can significantly enhance user experience, increase engagement, and boost user retention. In this chapter, we will explore the intricacies of designing user interfaces in Swift, leveraging SwiftUI, and UIKit, Apple's powerful frameworks designed for building UIs for iOS, macOS, watchOS, andtvOS applications.

We will cover best practices, essential components, and the tools available within Xcode to help you create an effective UI that meets user needs and enhances usability.

1. Understanding SwiftUI and UIKit

Before diving into the UI design process, it's crucial to understand the two primary frameworks used forbuilding interfaces in Swift.

1.1 SwiftUI

SwiftUI is a modern UI toolkit introduced by Apple that allows developers to create user interfaces across allApple platforms using a declarative syntax. SwiftUI simplifies UI design by allowing you to build interfaces by stacking elements in a hierarchy and having the framework automatically handle updates as data changes.

Key Features of SwiftUI:

Declarative Syntax: Build user interfaces by declaring what your UI should look like in a simple andexpressive way.

Live Previews: Utilize Xcode's canvas to see live previews of your UI while coding, enabling rapid prototyping and easier adjustments.

Adaptive Layouts: Create layouts that adapt to different screen sizes and orientations automatically.

Integration with Combine: Use the Combine framework to handle asynchronous data streams, making it easier to manage state changes in your UI.

1.2 UIKit

UIKit is the traditional framework for building iOS user interfaces. Although it is more extensive and can handle more complex scenarios than SwiftUI, UIKit employs an imperative programming style, which may feel more familiar to developers with experience in Objective-C or earlier Swift versions.

Key Features of UIKit:

Extensive Control Set: A rich set of UI elements like buttons, labels, tables, and collection views to create complex interfaces.

Storyboard Support: Visual interface builder that allows developers to design interfaces graphically.

Legacy Support: Support for older versions of iOS, making it necessary for projects that need backward compatibility.

2. Getting Started with SwiftUI

In this section, we will build a simple user interface using SwiftUI.### 2.1 Setting Up Your Xcode Project
Open Xcode and create a new project.
Choose the "App" template and ensure "SwiftUI" is selected as the interface option.
Name your project (e.g., "SwiftUIExample") and select a suitable location to save it.### 2.2 Creating Your First SwiftUI View
Open `ContentView.swift`, which is generated by default in a new SwiftUI project. It already contains a simple UI. Here's how you can customize it.

```swift
import SwiftUI

struct ContentView: View {var body: some View {
VStack {
Text("Welcome to SwiftUI")
.font(.largeTitle)
.padding() Button(action: {
// Button action here
}) {
Text("Press Me")
.font(.headline)
.padding()
.background(Color.blue)
.foregroundColor(.white)
.cornerRadius(10)
}
}
```

```
}
}
```

2.3 Adding States and Bindings

User interfaces often change based on user interactions. You can use state variables to manage dynamiccontent.

```swift
struct ContentView: View { @State private var count: Int =
0

var body: some View {VStack {
Text("You've pressed the button \(count) times")
.font(.title)
.padding() Button(action: {count += 1
}) {

Text("Press Me")
.padding()
.background(Color.green)
.foregroundColor(.white)
.cornerRadius(10)
}
}
.padding()
}
}
```

3. Creating User Interfaces with UIKit

Next, we'll look at how to create a user interface using UIKit.### 3.1 Setting Up Your Xcode Project
Create a new project and select the "App" template.
Choose UIKit as your interface option this time.### 3.2 Building a Simple UI
Open `Main.storyboard`, where you can drag and drop UI components. For instance, you can add a label and a button.

Drag a `UILabel` and a `UIButton` onto the view controller in the storyboard.
Control-drag from the button to the `ViewController.swift` file to create an IBOutlet and an IBAction.### 3.3 Handling Button Actions
In the `ViewController.swift`, you can implement the button's action.

```swift
class ViewController: UIViewController { @IBOutlet weak var counterLabel: UILabel!var count: Int = 0

override func viewDidLoad() {super.viewDidLoad()
counterLabel.text = "You've pressed the button \(count) times"
}

@IBAction func buttonPressed(_ sender: UIButton) {
count += 1
counterLabel.text = "You've pressed the button \(count) times"
}
}
```

4. Best Practices for UI Design

Creating a great user interface involves following best practices that enhance usability and accessibility.

4.1 Consistency

Maintain a consistent design throughout your application. Use uniform colors, fonts, and sizes to ensure users can navigate your app intuitively.

4.2 Accessibility

Ensure your app is accessible to all users, including those with disabilities. Use semantic labels, provide voice-over descriptions, and support dynamic type for text sizing.

4.3 Responsive Design

Design your UI to adapt to various screen sizes and orientations. Use Auto Layout in UIKit or adaptivity features in SwiftUI to ensure your views look great on every device.

4.4 User Feedback

Incorporate feedback mechanisms such as animations or alerts to inform users of actions taken within the app. This helps to create a more engaging experience.

Designing a user interface in Swift involves a blend of understanding both SwiftUI and UIKit, implementing best design practices, and utilizing the powerful tools provided by Xcode. As you continue to develop your skills, remember that user interface design is an iterative process that benefits greatly from user feedback and consistent testing.

Using Interface Builder

This chapter will guide you through the fundamental features of Interface Builder, how to incorporate it into your Swift projects, and how to bridge the gap between visual design and code through storyboards and XIB files.

1. Getting Started with Interface Builder

To begin using Interface Builder, you will first need to create a new Swift project in Xcode. Here's how to do it:

Open Xcode and select "Create a new Xcode project."
Choose iOS > App and click "Next."
Enter a product name, organization identifier, and select Swift as the language. Ensure "Use Storyboards" is checked.
Choose where to save your project and click "Create." ### Navigating Interface Builder
Once your project is created, you will automatically be taken to the Main.storyboard file, which is where you'll design your interface.

View Controller: The central element of the interface. Each screen of your application is represented by a View Controller.

Scene: A container for a View Controller and its interface elements. You can have multiple scenes in a storyboard, allowing for simple navigation flows.
Component Library: On the right side, you can find UI components to drag and drop into your scene, such as buttons, labels, image views, etc.

2. Designing Your Interface ### Adding UI Elements
To add UI elements to your View Controller:

Open the Component Library by clicking the "+" icon in the top right corner of Xcode.
Use the search bar or browse categories to find the elements you want.
Drag elements onto your View Controller scene. Resize and position them as necessary. ### Configuring Properties
Each UI element has customizable properties that you can modify in the Attributes Inspector:

Text: Change the text of UILabels, UIButtons, etc.
Color: Alter the background color and text color to match your design.
Font: Choose different fonts and styles to enhance the UI. ### Using Auto Layout
To ensure your UI is responsive across different devices and orientations, you need to make use of Auto Layout:

Select an element and click on the "Add New Constraints" icon (the square with lines).
Set constraints for leading, trailing, top, and bottom margins.
Use the "Resolve Auto Layout Issues" button to help

144

troubleshoot any layout conflicts. ### Creating Outlets and Actions
Once your UI is laid out, connecting interface elements to your Swift code requires the creation of outlets and actions:

Creating an Outlet: Hold down the `Control` key and drag from a UI element to your ViewController.swift file. Release to create a property, allowing you to reference the element in your code.
Creating an Action: Similar to creating an outlet, hold `Control` and drag from a UIButton to the code file, but then select "Action" to create a method that will be triggered upon interaction with the button.

Here's an example of what your code might look like after creating an outlet and an action for a button.

```swift
import UIKit

class ViewController: UIViewController {@IBOutlet weak var myLabel: UILabel!
@IBAction func buttonTapped(_ sender: UIButton) {
myLabel.text = "Button was tapped!"
}

override func viewDidLoad() {super.viewDidLoad()
}
}
```

3. Navigating Between View Controllers

In many applications, you will need to move from one view controller to another, such as transitioning from a login screen to a main menu.

Segues

Segues are the way to transition between view controllers in a storyboard. To create a segue:

Control-drag from a UI element (like a button) to another View Controller in your storyboard.
Choose the type of segue from the pop-up: Show, Modal, etc.
Give the segue an identifier in the Attributes Inspector so that you can reference it in your code. ### Performing Segues Programmatically
In your code, you can also perform segues programmatically:

```swift
override func prepare(for segue: UIStoryboardSegue, sender: Any?) { if segue.identifier == "yourSegueIdentifier" {
let destinationVC = segue.destination as! DestinationViewController
// Pass data to the new view controller if needed
}
}
```

4. Using XIB Files

Besides storyboards, XIB files are another way to create

user interfaces in Xcode:

Create a new XIB file by going to File > New > File and selecting User Interface > View.
Design your UI in the XIB just as you would in a storyboard, and set up outlets and actions similarly.
You will load the XIB in your ViewController's code when you want to present it.

```swift
guard let view = Bundle.main.loadNibNamed("MyCustomView", owner: self, options: nil)?.first as? MyCustomView else { return }
self.view.addSubview(view)
```

By mastering Interface Builder, you can create visually appealing and responsive UIs while enhancing the efficiency of your development workflow. As you grow more comfortable with Auto Layout, segues, and the integration of code, you'll find that the power of Swift combined with Interface Builder allows for both impressive creativity and robust functionality in your applications.

Auto Layout and Constraints

Auto Layout is a powerful system in Swift that helps developers achieve this flexibility by allowing them to define how views relate to one another and to their containers. In this chapter, we will explore the fundamentals of Auto Layout, discuss constraints and their application, and examine best practices for implementing Auto Layout in Swift.
Understanding Auto Layout ### What is Auto Layout? Auto Layout is a layout system that enables developers to create user interfaces that automatically adjust to different screen sizes and device orientations. Unlike traditional layout methods, which rely on fixed frames, Auto Layout uses rules or "constraints" to define how views are positioned relative to one another and their superviews.

Key Concepts
To effectively use Auto Layout, it's essential to understand a few key concepts:

Views and Superviews: In the view hierarchy, views are nested within other views. The parent view is known as the superview.

Constraints: Constraints are rules that dictate how views should be laid out in relation to each other. These can specify size, position, alignment, and spacing.

Intrinsic Content Size: Some views have a natural size based on their content (e.g., UILabel). This size is known as the intrinsic content size and can be taken into account

148

when applying constraints.

Priorities: Constraints have priorities that indicate their importance. This is useful when there's potential for conflicts between constraints.

Content Hugging and Compression Resistance: These properties control how views respond to changes in size: hugging determines how tightly a view wants to fit around its content, while compression resistance defines how well a view resists being made smaller than its intrinsic size.

Setting Up Auto Layout ### Using Interface Builder

While Auto Layout can be effectively implemented programmatically, Apple provides an intuitive graphical tool, Interface Builder, in Xcode. Here's how to set up Auto Layout constraints using Interface Builder:

Open your storyboard or XIB file.
Select the view or control you want to constrain.
Click on the "Add New Constraints" button in the bottom right.
Enter the required spacing values and check the boxes for the sides you want to constrain.
Click "Add Constraints."

Your constraints will appear in the document outline, where you can edit, activate, or deactivate them as necessary.

Programmatic Constraints

For more control or complex layouts, you might prefer to implement Auto Layout in code. Here's a simple example to demonstrate how to add constraints programmatically:

149

```swift
import UIKit
class MyViewController: UIViewController {let myView:
UIView = {
let view = UIView()
view.backgroundColor = .bluereturn view
}()

override func viewDidLoad() {super.viewDidLoad()

view.addSubview(myView)

myView.translatesAutoresizingMaskIntoConstraints    =
falseNSLayoutConstraint.activate([
myView.widthAnchor.constraint(equalToConstant: 100),
myView.heightAnchor.constraint(equalToConstant: 100),
myView.centerXAnchor.constraint(equalTo:
view.centerXAnchor),
myView.centerYAnchor.constraint(equalTo:
view.centerYAnchor)
])
}
}
```

In this example, we create a blue square view and center it
within its parent view using Auto Layoutconstraints. We
set   `translatesAutoresizingMaskIntoConstraints`   to
`false` to prevent the view from generating its constraints
automatically.
Working with Constraints ### Activation and
Deactivation
You can dynamically manage constraints by activating or

deactivating them. This is particularly useful when responding to user interactions or layout changes. Here's how you can activate and deactivate constraints:

```swift
// Assuming we have an array of constraints
var constraintsArray: [NSLayoutConstraint] = []

// Adding constraints
constraintsArray.append(myView.widthAnchor.constraint(equalToConstant: 100))
constraintsArray.append(myView.heightAnchor.constraint(equalToConstant: 100))
NSLayoutConstraint.activate(constraintsArray)

// Deactivating constraints
NSLayoutConstraint.deactivate(constraintsArray)
```

Handling Conflicts
When you create conflicting constraints, Auto Layout will try to resolve them based on the priorities you set. It's essential to ensure that your constraints logically make sense. You can debug conflicts using Xcode's View Debugger or by checking the console output for Auto Layout warnings.## Best Practices for Using Auto Layout
Avoid Magic Numbers: Always use constants or calculated expressions for dimensions and spacingsrather than hard coding them.

Keep Constraints Simple: Aim for simplicity in your constraint relationships to reduce potential conflicts and improve readability.

Use Stack Views: Stack views simplify layout management by automatically handling the positioning and sizing of their arranged subviews.

Leverage View Hierarchies: Organize your views into reusable components or views to maintain a cleaner codebase.

Test on Multiple Devices: Regularly test your layout on various devices and orientations to ensure that it behaves as intended under different conditions.

Auto Layout is an essential part of building responsive, adaptive user interfaces in Swift. By understanding constraints, how to set them up, and implementing best practices, you can create interfaces that not only look good but also provide a seamless experience across devices. In the next chapter, we will delve into stack views and how they can be leveraged to simplify layout management further.

Chapter 10: Connecting UI to Code

This chapter delves into the various techniques used in Swift to connect UI components designed in Interface Builder with the underlying code, ensuring a seamless user experience. We will explore outlet connections, action methods, and the concept of target-action to facilitate this integration.

10.1 Setting up the User Interface

Before we dive into the code, let's outline a simple user interface using Xcode's Interface Builder, which will serve as our foundation. Follow these steps to create a basic UI:

Open Xcode: Create a new project and select a Single View App.
Design the Interface:
Open `Main.storyboard`.
Drag a UILabel to the center of the screen and change its text to "Hello, World!".
Add a UIButton below the label and set its title to "Press Me".
Set the Constraints: Use Auto Layout to center the label and button, ensuring they look good on all device sizes.

Now that we have a basic UI set up, let's connect these elements to our Swift code.## 10.2 Creating Outlets
Outlets in Swift allow your code to reference UI elements. To create an outlet:

Open the Assistant Editor: With your storyboard

open, click on the `Assistant Editor` button in theXcode toolbar.
Create an Outlet:
Control-drag from the UILabel in your storyboard to the `ViewController.swift` file.
When prompted, name your outlet (e.g., `greetingLabel`), and ensure it is marked with `@IBOutlet`. Thissignifies that it is an interface element linked to your code.

Here is how the code would look after creating an outlet:

```swift
import UIKit
class ViewController: UIViewController { @IBOutlet weak var greetingLabel: UILabel!override func viewDidLoad() {
super.viewDidLoad()
// Initial setup
}
}
```

10.3 Creating Actions

Actions are methods that are triggered in response to user interactions with UI elements. To create an actionfor your button:

Control-drag from the UIButton in your storyboard to the `ViewController.swift` file.
Configure the Action: Name the action (e.g., `buttonPressed`) and ensure it is marked with `@IBAction`. This will link the UIButton's tap event to this method.Here is an example of how your action might look:

```swift
@IBAction func buttonPressed(_ sender: UIButton) {
greetingLabel.text = "Button Pressed!"
}
```

10.4 The Target-Action Pattern

The target-action pattern is an essential concept in UIKit that allows you to respond to events from UI controls. When you set up an action, you are essentially defining a target (in this case, your
`ViewController`) that will handle specific actions (like pressing a button).

By default, the UIButton implements the target-action design pattern. When you call
`addTarget(_:action:for:)` method, you establish which method to call when a specific event occurs. This can also be done programmatically:

```swift
override func viewDidLoad() {super.viewDidLoad()
// Programmatic UI setup
let button = UIButton(type: .system)
button.setTitle("Press Me", for: .normal)
button.addTarget(self, action: #selector(buttonPressed(_:)), for: .touchUpInside)
view.addSubview(button)
}
```

In this case, the `buttonPressed(_:)` method will be

called whenever the button is tapped. ## 10.5 Updating the UI in Response to Model Changes

As your application grows, you may want to update the UI based on changes in your data models. This can be accomplished by utilizing properties and methods to manipulate the UI. For instance, if you had a data model representing a user's state, you could observe those changes and update the UI accordingly:

```swift
var userName: String? {didSet {
greetingLabel.text = "Hello, \(userName ?? "World!")"
}
}
```

Here, whenever `userName` is assigned a new value, the label will automatically update to reflect that change.

Connecting UI elements to your Swift code is a foundational skill in iOS development that empowers you to create dynamic and interactive apps. By understanding how to create outlets, actions, and leverage the target-action pattern, you can build interfaces that respond intuitively to user input. As you continue your journey, keep experimenting with more complex UI elements and behaviors, allowing your applications to achieve deeper levels of interactivity and user engagement.

Outlets and Actions

In Swift, a powerful and intuitive programming language developed by Apple, managing user interface elements efficiently relies on two crucial concepts: outlets and actions. This chapter explores these concepts, their functionalities, and how to implement them in your iOS applications with Swift.

Understanding Outlets

Outlets are a way to connect UI elements defined in Interface Builder (IB) to your Swift code. By creating an outlet, you can interact programmatically with UI components such as labels, buttons, image views, and more. Outlets allow for greater flexibility and control over your user interface, enabling developers to manipulate properties and respond to user interactions dynamically.

Creating Outlets

To create an outlet, follow these steps:

Open the Interface Builder: Open your storyboard or XIB file in Xcode.

Select the UI Element: Click on the UI element you want to create an outlet for. For example, you may select a `UILabel` or `UIButton`.

Open the Assistant Editor: This splits your view, showing both the Interface Builder and the associated Swift file side by side.

Control-Drag to Swift Code: Press and hold the "Control" key, then drag from the UI element to the Swift code file. Release the mouse button once you reach the desired location in your class. A pop-up will appear, prompting you to name the outlet.

Name the Outlet: Provide a meaningful name for the outlet (e.g., `labelTitle`) and ensure the connection type is set to "Outlet."

Create the Connection: Click "Connect" to create the outlet. You should see a new line of code generated in your class, resembling the following example:

```swift
@IBOutlet weak var labelTitle: UILabel!
```

Working with Outlets

Once you have created an outlet, you can manipulate the UI element from your Swift code. For example, you can change the text of a UILabel or alter the background color of a UIButton:

```swift
override func viewDidLoad() {super.viewDidLoad()

// Set the text of the label
labelTitle.text = "Welcome to Swift Programming!"
}
```

Using outlets allows developers to create dynamic interfaces that react to application logic, making the user experience more interactive and engaging.

Understanding Actions

Actions are another critical aspect of the iOS user interface framework. They allow your code to respond to user interactions, such as button taps or other gestures. An action serves as a bridge between the user interface and the code, capturing events triggered by the user.

Creating Actions

Creating actions in Swift can be accomplished through a process similar to that of outlets:

Select the UI Element: In the Interface Builder, select the UI element for which you want to create an action,

159

typically a button.

Open the Assistant Editor: Just as before, open the Assistant Editor to view your Swift file.

Control-Drag to Swift Code: Control-drag from the UI element (e.g., a UIButton) to your Swift file.

Name the Action: In the pop-up, choose "Action" as the connection type and give your action a meaningful name (e.g., `buttonPressed`).

Choose the Event: By default, the action will be connected to the "Touch Up Inside" event, which is commonly used for buttons. You can also select other events (e.g., "Touch Down" or "Value Changed" for switch controls).

Connect the Action: Click "Connect" to generate the action method, which will look like this:

```swift
@IBAction func buttonPressed(_ sender: UIButton) {
// Action code goes here
}
```

Implementing the Action

With the action set up, you can now define what happens when the user interacts with the UI element. Here's an example of how to implement an action to change the label text when the button is pressed:

```swift
@IBAction func buttonPressed(_ sender: UIButton) {
labelTitle.text = "Button was pressed!"
}
```

In this snippet, whenever the button is tapped, the text of the label will change, thus providing feedback to the user.

The Importance of Outlets and Actions

Understanding outlets and actions is fundamental for any iOS developer using Swift. These features enable:

Separation of Concerns: By connecting UI elements to the code, developers can maintain a clear separation between interface design and functionality.
Dynamic User Interfaces: With the ability to manipulate UI elements through outlets and respond to user inputs via actions, developers can create dynamic interfaces that enhance user engagement.
Maintainability: Outlets and actions help in organizing code better, making it easier to maintain and update the application as it grows in complexity.

As you continue your journey in app development, mastering these fundamental concepts will empower you to craft applications that are not only visually appealing but also highly functional and user-friendly.
Through practice and experimentation, you will find yourself increasingly adept at building responsive interfaces that meet the demands of modern users.

Responding to User Interactions

In Swift, Apple's powerful programming language for iOS, macOS, watchOS, and tvOS development, developers have a vast array of tools and frameworks at their disposal. This chapter will explore the various ways to capture and respond to user interactions in Swift, focusing on gesture recognizers, UI controls, and how to tailor responses to enhance user engagement.

Understanding User Interactions

User interactions encompass a wide range of activities including taps, swipes, pinches, and presses. Understanding how to recognize and handle these interactions is fundamental for building intuitive and responsive user interfaces. In Swift, we leverage UIKit, the foundational framework for iOS applications, which provides numerous classes and methods for interacting with users.

Gesture Recognizers

Gesture recognizers are powerful tools in Swift that allow you to recognize user gestures and respond accordingly. They are crucial for making apps more interactive without the need for complicated touch-handling code. Here are the most commonly used gesture recognizers:

Tap Gesture Recognizer

A tap gesture recognizer detects when a user taps the screen. Here's how to implement a tap gesture recognizer in Swift:

```swift
import UIKit

class ViewController: UIViewController { override func viewDidLoad() {
super.viewDidLoad()

let tapGesture = UITapGestureRecognizer(target: self, action: #selector(handleTap(_:)))
view.addGestureRecognizer(tapGesture)
}

@objc func handleTap(_ sender: UITapGestureRecognizer) {print("View tapped!")
}
}
```

In this example, when the user taps the view, the `handleTap` method is called, allowing us to define the app's response.

Long Press Gesture Recognizer

Long press gestures can be useful for providing additional options or actions when the user interacts with a control. Here's an example of how to use a long press gesture recognizer:

```swift
let                 longPressGesture              =
UILongPressGestureRecognizer(target:      self,     action:
#selector(handleLongPress(_:)))
view.addGestureRecognizer(longPressGesture)

@objc        func        handleLongPress(_       sender:
UILongPressGestureRecognizer)  {  if  sender.state  ==
.began {
print("Long pressed!")
}
}
```

In this case, the app responds differently based on the state of the gesture recognizer, allowing for nuanced interaction.

Swipe Gesture Recognizer

Swipe gestures enable actions such as navigation between views or performing relative actions. Here's an implementation for a swipe gesture:

```swift
let swipeGesture = UISwipeGestureRecognizer(target:
self,       action:        #selector(handleSwipe(_:)))
view.addGestureRecognizer(swipeGesture)

@objc       func       handleSwipe(_       sender:
UISwipeGestureRecognizer) {print("Swiped!")
}
```

By combining these gesture recognizers, you can create a rich and interactive user experience.## Responding to UI Controls

In addition to gesture recognizers, UIKit provides numerous UI controls such as buttons, switches, sliders, and more. Each control has its own way of responding to user interactions, usually through the use of target-action pairs or delegates.

UIButton

For instance, a `UIButton` can be set up to respond when a user taps it:

```swift
let button = UIButton(type: .system) button.setTitle("Tap Me", for: .normal)
button.addTarget(self, action: #selector(buttonTapped), for: .touchUpInside)

@objc func buttonTapped() {print("Button tapped!")
}
```

UISwitch

Similarly, a `UISwitch` offers an efficient way to capture on/off toggling actions:

```swift
let switchControl = UISwitch()
switchControl.addTarget(self,                            action:
```

```swift
#selector(switchChanged(_:)), for: .valueChanged)

@objc func switchChanged(_ sender: UISwitch) { if
sender.isOn {
print("Switch is ON")
} else {
print("Switch is OFF")
}
}
```

UISlider

The `UISlider` allows users to select a value from a range,
and responding to its changes can enhance functionality:

```swift
let slider = UISlider()
slider.addTarget(self,                               action:
#selector(sliderValueChanged(_:)), for: .valueChanged)

@objc func sliderValueChanged(_ sender: UISlider) {
print("Slider value: \(sender.value)")
}
```

Custom Touch Handling

In cases where predefined controls and gesture
recognizers do not suffice, you can implement custom
touchhandling by overriding touch methods in your view
or view controller.

```swift
class CustomView: UIView {
override func touchesBegan(_ touches: Set<UITouch>,
with event: UIEvent?) { print("Touch began at:
\(touches.first?.location(in: self) ?? CGPoint.zero)")
}
}
```

This method gives you full control over how to respond to user touches, making it suitable for custom views or specialized interactions.

By using gesture recognizers, UI controls, and custom touch handling, developers can craft a rich user experience that responds intuitively to user input. The examples provided throughout this chapter offer a solid foundation for building your own interactive applications, paving the way toward developing sophisticated user interfaces in your Swift projects.

Chapter 11: Working with Data

Swift, Apple's powerful and intuitive programming language, provides robust tools and frameworks for working with data, making it easier for developers to handle complex data structures and manage persistent storage. In this chapter, we will explore various aspects of working with data in Swift, including data types, serialization, persistence, and networking.

11.1 Understanding Data Types

At the core of any programming language are its data types. Swift offers a rich set of data types that cater to different needs. The primary categories include:

11.1.1 Basic Data Types

Integers: Swift supports both signed (`Int`) and unsigned integers (`UInt`). The `Int` type adjusts its size based on the platform (32-bit or 64-bit).

Floating-Point Numbers: Use `Float` for single-precision data and `Double` for double-precision. Swift's type system ensures type safety during mathematical operations.

Booleans: The `Bool` type represents `true` or `false` values, making it essential for conditional logic.

Strings: Swift provides a powerful `String` type for textual data, supporting Unicode and various string manipulation features.

Collections: Swift has three primary collection types: `Array`, `Dictionary`, and `Set`. These types allow for storing multiple values in a single structure.

11.1.2 Optionals

In Swift, a variable can either have a value or not, which is indicated by the use of optionals. An optional is a type that can hold either a value or `nil`, enabling developers to implement safe handling of missing data.
For instance, `String?` can contain a string or be `nil`.

```swift
var name: String? = "Alice"
name = nil // This is perfectly acceptable
```

Using optionals effectively can lead to safer, more robust code.## 11.2 Data Serialization
Serialization is the process of converting data into a format that can be easily stored or transmitted and reconstructed later. Swift offers several ways to serialize and deserialize data, with the most popular being JSON (JavaScript Object Notation).

11.2.1 Working with JSON

Swift provides a built-in `Codable` protocol that combines the functionalities of `Encodable` and `Decodable`. This makes it incredibly simple to encode and decode JSON data. #### Example: Encoding and Decoding JSON

Consider a simple struct representing a `User`:

```swift
struct User: Codable {let name: String
let age: Int
}
```

To encode a `User` instance into JSON:

```swift
let user = User(name: "Alice", age: 30)
if let jsonData = try? JSONEncoder().encode(user) {
// jsonData contains the JSON representation of the user
}
```

To decode JSON back into a `User` object:

```swift
if let decodedUser = try? JSONDecoder().decode(User.self, from: jsonData) {
print(decodedUser.name) // Output: Alice
}
```

This powerful serialization approach minimizes the need for manual data parsing, reducing boilerplate code and potential errors.

11.3 Data Persistence

Persistence is crucial for applications that require data to be saved between app launches. Swift offers several methods for data persistence, including UserDefaults, File System, and Core Data.

11.3.1 UserDefaults

For small pieces of data, such as user preferences, UserDefaults is often the easiest solution.

```swift
let defaults = UserDefaults.standard defaults.set("Alice", forKey: "username")

if let username = defaults.string(forKey: "username") {
print(username) // Output: Alice
}
```

11.3.2 File System

When dealing with larger datasets or files, the file system is more suitable. Swift provides methods for reading and writing files, allowing developers to manage data efficiently.

```swift
let filePath = "/path/to/file.txt"let text = "Hello, World!"
do {
```

```
try text.write(toFile: filePath, atomically: true, encoding:
.utf8)
} catch {
print("Error writing file: \(error)")
}
```

11.3.3 Core Data

For complex data models and relationships, Core Data is
the go-to solution. It provides an object graph
management and persistence framework, allowing
developers to interact with data in an object-oriented way.

```swift
import CoreData

class UserEntity: NSManagedObject { @NSManaged var
name: String @NSManaged var age: Int16
}

// Example of saving a User
let userEntity = UserEntity(context: managedContext)
userEntity.name = "Alice"
userEntity.age = 30do {
try managedContext.save()
} catch {
print("Failed saving: \(error)")
}
```

11.4 Networking and Data Retrieval

172

In the world of web applications, fetching data from APIs is a common requirement. Swift's `URLSession` is the primary class used for making network requests.

11.4.1 Making Requests

```swift
let url = URL(string: "https://api.example.com/user")!
let task = URLSession.shared.dataTask(with: url) { data, response, error inguard let data = data, error == nil else {
print("Error: \(error!)")return
}

let decoder = JSONDecoder()
if let user = try? decoder.decode(User.self, from: data) {

print(user.name)
}
}
task.resume()
```

Using `URLSession`, you can make GET, POST, PUT, and DELETE requests to interact with web APIsseamlessly.

11.4.2 Handling Errors

Error handling is vital in network operations. Swift's `Result` type can be used to manage outcomes neatly:

```swift
enum NetworkError: Error {case badURL
case serverError
```

```
}
```
```
```

By adopting Swift's error handling strategies, you can build more resilient applications that handle data interactions gracefully.

In this chapter, we've laid the groundwork for understanding how to work with data in Swift. From basic data types to advanced serialization, persistence, and networking, Swift provides a comprehensive suite of tools for managing data effectively.

Using Arrays and Dictionaries

Two of the foundational data structures in Swift are Arrays and Dictionaries. In this chapter, we will explore how to use these structures, their characteristics, and some practical examples to help you understand their functionalities.

1. Understanding Arrays

Arrays in Swift are ordered collections of values. They can store multiple values of the same type, and you can access each element using an index. Here are some key features of arrays in Swift:

Homogeneous: All elements in an array must be of the same type, which ensures type safety.
Ordered: The elements in an array are stored in a specific order, which can be retrieved using their indices

(starting from 0).
Dynamic Size: Arrays can grow or shrink as needed; you can add or remove elements at any time. ### 1.1 Creating Arrays
To create an array, you can use the array literal syntax or the `Array` initializer. Below are examples of both methods:

```swift
// Using array literal syntax
var fruits = ["Apple", "Banana", "Cherry"]

// Using Array initializer
var vegetables: [String] = Array(repeating: "Carrot", count: 3)
```

1.2 Accessing and Modifying Arrays

Accessing elements in an array is straightforward. You can use subscript syntax:

```swift
let firstFruit = fruits[0] // "Apple"
```

Modifying arrays can be done using methods like `append`, `insert`, and `remove`:

```swift
// Adding an element
fruits.append("Date") // Array becomes ["Apple", "Banana", "Cherry", "Date"]
```

```
// Inserting an element
fruits.insert("Blueberry", at: 1) // Array becomes ["Apple",
"Blueberry", "Banana", "Cherry", "Date"]

// Removing an element
fruits.remove(at: 2) // Array becomes ["Apple",
"Blueberry", "Cherry", "Date"]
```

1.3 Iterating Over Arrays

You can easily loop through arrays using a `for` loop or
the `forEach` method:

```swift
for fruit in fruits {print(fruit)
}

// Using forEach fruits.forEach { fruit in
print(fruit)
}
```

2. Understanding Dictionaries

Dictionaries are unordered collections of key-value pairs.
Each key in a dictionary must be unique, and values can be
of any type. Here are some key features of dictionaries in
Swift:

Unordered: Unlike arrays, the order of key-value
pairs in a dictionary is not guaranteed.

176

Keys and Values: Each value is associated with a unique key, which you use to access the value.
Dynamic Size: Similar to arrays, dictionaries can grow or shrink dynamically.### 2.1 Creating Dictionaries
You can create a dictionary using an initializer or by using dictionary literal syntax:

```swift
// Using dictionary literal syntax
var cityPopulation = ["New York": 8419600, "Los Angeles": 3980400, "Chicago": 2716000]

// Using Dictionary initializer
var countryCodes: [String: String] = Dictionary(uniqueKeysWithValues: [("US", "United States"), ("CA","Canada")])
```

2.2 Accessing and Modifying Dictionaries

Accessing values in a dictionary is done using subscript syntax with the key:

```swift
let nyPopulation = cityPopulation["New York"] // Optional(8419600)
```

To modify the dictionary, you can add new key-value pairs, update existing pairs, or remove them:

```swift
// Adding a new entry cityPopulation["Houston"] =
```

2328000

```
// Updating an existing entry cityPopulation["Chicago"] = 2706000

// Removing an entry
cityPopulation.removeValue(forKey: "Los Angeles")
```

2.3 Iterating Over Dictionaries

You can loop through the key-value pairs in a dictionary using a `for` loop or the `forEach` method:

```swift
for (city, population) in cityPopulation { print("\(city): \(population) people")
}

// Using forEach
cityPopulation.forEach { (city, population) in
print("\(city): \(population) people")
}
```

3. Arrays and Dictionaries: Practical Examples

Let's put our knowledge to use with some practical scenarios that combine arrays and dictionaries. ### 3.1 Example: Managing a List of Students
Suppose we want to maintain a list of students and their grades. We can use an array of dictionaries for this purpose:

```swift
var students: [[String: Any]] = [ ["name": "Alice", "grade":
85],
["name": "Bob", "grade": 92],
["name": "Charlie", "grade": 78]
]

// Adding a new student students.append(["name":
"David", "grade": 88])

// Updating a student's grade
if let index = students.firstIndex(where: { $0["name"] as?
String == "Alice" }) {students[index]["grade"] = 90
}

// Printing student names and grades for student in
students {
if let name = student["name"], let grade =
student["grade"] {print("\(name): \(grade)")
}
}
```

3.2 Example: Counting Votes

Imagine we are counting votes for a poll. We can use a
dictionary where keys are candidates' names and values
are the number of votes each candidate has received:

```swift
var votes: [String: Int] = [:]
```

```
// Voting process
let candidates = ["Alice", "Bob", "Charlie"]for candidate in
candidates {
votes[candidate, default: 0] += 1 // Suppose each
candidate gets one vote
}

// Display results
for (candidate, voteCount) in votes { print("\(candidate)
received \(voteCount) votes.")
}
```
` ` `

We covered how to create, modify, and access elements
within these structures and saw practical examples that
illustrate their usefulness in real-world scenarios.
Mastering arrays and dictionaries will greatly enhance
your ability to handle data in Swift applications. Upon
understanding these concepts, you can confidently move
on to more complex data structures and algorithms,
expanding your capabilities as a Swift developer.

Persisting Data with User Defaults

In the realm of iOS application development, managing
user preferences and small amounts of data is a common
requirement. User Defaults is a powerful feature provided
by Apple that allows developers to storesimple data types
persistently. This chapter explores how to utilize User
Defaults effectively in Swift, providing a reliable way to
save and retrieve user settings and preferences.

What is User Defaults?

User Defaults is part of the Foundation framework in iOS, macOS, tvOS, and watchOS. It offers a simple interface to store key-value pairs persistently. It is particularly suited for storing user preferences like settings, configurations, or any small piece of data that should persist between app launches.

Key Features of User Defaults:

Simple Key-Value Storage: User Defaults is ideal for lightweight data.
Automatic Serialization: Data types such as Strings, Numbers, Booleans, Dates, and Data can be stored without additional serialization steps.
Synchronous Storage: While basic operations are fast, it's important to note that User Defaults reads and writes are synchronous, which means they can block the main thread if you're working with large datasets or performing frequent operations.

Setting Up User Defaults in Swift ### Importing Foundation
Before you start working with User Defaults, ensure you have imported the Foundation framework in your Swift file:

```swift
import Foundation
```

Storing Data

To store data in User Defaults, you can access the shared instance of `UserDefaults` using the `standard` property. This uses the code structure:

```swift
let defaults = UserDefaults.standard
```

Now let's explore how to store various data types. #### Storing Strings
```swift
let username = "john_doe" defaults.set(username, forKey: "username")
```

Storing Integers

```swift
let userAge = 28
defaults.set(userAge, forKey: "userAge")
```

Storing Booleans

```swift
let isSubscribed = true
defaults.set(isSubscribed, forKey: "isSubscribed")
```

Storing Arrays

```swift
let favoriteColors = ["Red", "Blue", "Green"]
defaults.set(favoriteColors, forKey: "favoriteColors")
```

Retrieving Data

Retrieving data from User Defaults involves using the same key you used to store the value. Here's how you can retrieve different data types:

Retrieving Strings

```swift
if let storedUsername = defaults.string(forKey: "username") { print("Stored Username: \(storedUsername)")
}
```

Retrieving Integers

```swift
let storedAge = defaults.integer(forKey: "userAge")
print("Stored Age: \(storedAge)")
```

Retrieving Booleans

```swift
let isUserSubscribed = defaults.bool(forKey: "isSubscribed") print("Is User Subscribed: \(isUserSubscribed)")
```

183

```
```

Retrieving Arrays

```swift
if let colors = defaults.stringArray(forKey:
"favoriteColors") { print("Favorite Colors:
\(colors.joined(separator: ", "))")
}
```

Updating Data

Updating data in User Defaults is as simple as storing it
again with the same key. When you call
`set(_:forKey:)` with the same key, it overwrites the
existing value.

```swift
let newUsername = "doe_john"
defaults.set(newUsername, forKey: "username") // This
will update the value
```

Removing Data

If you need to remove a specific entry from User Defaults,
you can use the `removeObject(forKey:)` method:

```swift
defaults.removeObject(forKey: "username")
```

Synchronizing User Defaults

User Defaults automatically synchronizes in the background, but if you need to ensure that the data is savedimmediately, you can call:

```swift
defaults.synchronize()
```

However, this method is generally not needed in modern iOS applications. ### Best Practices
Use Meaningful Keys: Always use descriptive keys for your data. This practice helps avoid clashesand improves code readability.

Limit the Use of User Defaults: User Defaults is not designed to store large amounts of data. For larger datasets, consider using a database (like Core Data or SQLite).

Type Safety: When retrieving values, always consider the optional nature of the returned data (e.g.,use `if let` or `guard` to safely unwrap).

Test Your Code: Regularly test the behavior of storing and retrieving data to ensure reliability,especially when updating or changing keys.

Data Migration: When updating your app, consider how changes to stored data structures will affectexisting users. Always implement a migration strategy when needed.

185

User Defaults is an invaluable tool when it comes to persisting simple user data in Swift applications. Its ease of use, combined with robust capabilities to store various data types, makes it an essential part of iOS development. By following best practices and understanding its limitations, developers can effectively utilize User Defaults to enhance user experience by remembering their preferences and configurations between app sessions.

Chapter 12: Networking and APIs

In the iOS ecosystem, Swift has emerged as a powerful language for network programming, offering a variety of tools and frameworks that simplify the process. This chapter will explore how to effectively handle networking and work with APIs in Swift, providing you with the knowledge and techniques to build responsive, data-driven applications.

12.1 Introduction to Networking in Swift

At its core, networking involves sending and receiving data over the internet. For iOS developers, understanding URL requests, response handling, and data parsing is essential. Swift offers several built-in tools to facilitate networking tasks, including `URLSession`, the fundamental class for making HTTP requests.

12.1.1 Understanding URLSession

`URLSession` is part of the Foundation framework and is used to create network requests. It provides an API for downloading and uploading data, managing cached responses, and authenticating requests. `URLSession` makes it simple to perform synchronous and asynchronous tasks without blocking the main thread.

12.1.2 Making HTTP Requests

Making a simple HTTP request in Swift using `URLSession` involves creating a `URL` instance, formulating a request, and handling the response. Below is a basic example of making a GET request to fetch data from an API.

```swift
```swift
import Foundation

func fetchData(from urlString: String) {
guard let url = URL(string: urlString) else { return }

let task = URLSession.shared.dataTask(with: url) { data, response, error in
// Handle error
if let error = error {
print("Error fetching data: \(error)")return
}

// Ensure response is valid
guard let httpResponse = response as? HTTPURLResponse,
(200...299).contains(httpResponse.statusCode) else {
print("Server error")return
}

// Process received dataif let data = data {
// Handle data
print(String(data: data, encoding: .utf8) ?? "Data unreadable")
```
```

```
    }
  }
  task.resume()
}
```

In the example above, a `dataTask` is created with a closure to handle the result of the request. Remember to call `resume()` to start the task, which runs asynchronously in the background.

12.2 Handling JSON Responses

Most modern APIs return data in JSON format, which is easy to work with in Swift. Swift's `Codable` protocol allows for seamless encoding and decoding of JSON data into custom structures.

12.2.1 Creating Models with Codable

To handle JSON, define a model that conforms to `Codable`. Below is an example of a simple model representing a user.

```swift
struct User: Codable {let id: Int
let name: String
let username: Stringlet email: String
}
```

12.2.2 Decoding JSON Data

Once you have the model, you can decode JSON data using `JSONDecoder`. Here's how you can modify the previous fetching function to decode the response into a `User` object array.

```swift
func fetchUsers() {
let                    urlString                    =
"https://jsonplaceholder.typicode.com/users"guard let url
= URL(string: urlString) else { return }

let task = URLSession.shared.dataTask(with: url) { data,
response, error iniflet error = error {
print("Error fetching users: \(error)")return
}
guard let data = data else { return }do {
let users = try JSONDecoder().decode([User].self, from:
data)print(users)
} catch {
print("Error decoding JSON: \(error)")
}
}
task.resume()
```

```
}
```

In the implementation above, we use `JSONDecoder` to decode an array of `User` objects directly from the response data.

12.3 Error Handling in Networking

Error handling is crucial when dealing with network requests. There are several types of errors you might encounter, including network connectivity issues, HTTP errors, and decoding errors. It's essential to provide meaningful error messages to help diagnose issues and improve user experience.

12.3.1 Custom Error Types

You can create custom error types to give more information about networking failures.

```swift
enum NetworkError: Error {case urlError
case requestFailed case serverError case decodingError
}
```

12.3.2 Enhanced Error Handling

Incorporate custom errors into your requests to manage failures more gracefully.

```swift
```

```swift
func fetchUsersWithErrorHandling() {
let                    urlString                 =
"https://jsonplaceholder.typicode.com/users"

guard  let  url  =  URL(string:  urlString)  else  {
print(NetworkError.urlError)
return
}

let task = URLSession.shared.dataTask(with: url) { data,
response, error iniflet error = error {
print("Request    error:    \(error.localizedDescription)")
return
}

guard   let   httpResponse   =   response   as?
HTTPURLResponse,
(200...299).contains(httpResponse.statusCode) else {
print(NetworkError.serverError)return
}

guard   let   data   =   data   else   {
print(NetworkError.requestFailed)return
}
```

```
do {
let users = try JSONDecoder().decode([User].self, from:
data)print(users)
} catch { print(NetworkError.decodingError)
}
}
task.resume()
}
```

12.4 Networking Best Practices

When working with networking in Swift, keeping best practices in mind can enhance your application's performance and reliability.

12.4.1 Use URLSession Configuration

`URLSession` provides the option to be configured for different behaviors such as background downloads, caching, and timeout settings. Use the shared session for simple tasks but consider creating a custom session for larger applications.

12.4.2 Manage Your Threads

Network calls are inherently asynchronous to avoid blocking the main thread. Always ensure that UI updates are performed on the main thread:

```swift
DispatchQueue.main.async {
// Update UI here
}
```

```
```

12.4.3 Caching and Performance

Use URLCache or third-party libraries (like Alamofire) to manage caching strategies effectively. This can drastically improve performance and provide a smoother user experience, especially in scenarios where data doesn't change frequently.

Networking and API integration are crucial skills for any iOS developer. Swift's networking capabilities, combined with the power of Codable for JSON parsing, make it easier than ever to connect applications with external data sources. By understanding the tools and best practices, developers can create robust and responsive applications that harness the full potential of the internet.

Making Network Requests

Whether you're building a simple app that fetches a JSON from a public API or complex applications that require multi-tier network interactions, understanding how to make network requests in Swift is crucial. This chapter will guide you through the principles and practices of performing network operations in Swift using URLSession, handling responses, parsing data, and managing errors.

Understanding URLSession

Swift provides the `URLSession` class that allows you to

create network requests. It is powerful and easy to use, encapsulating all the complexity of managing connections and data transmission.

Basic Components of URLSession

URL: Represents a web address. You create a URL using the `URL(string:)` initializer.
URLRequest: Encapsulates a URL load request. It allows you to configure the HTTP method, headers, body data, and more.
Data Task: A specific type of task that retrieves the contents of a URL and calls a completion handler upon completion.

Creating a Simple GET Request

Let's start with a simple example of making a GET request to retrieve JSON data from a public API. We will use the JSONPlaceholder API, a fake online REST API for testing and prototyping.

```swift
import Foundation

// URL of the API endpoint
let               urlString               =
"https://jsonplaceholder.typicode.com/posts/1"

// Create a URL instance
if let url = URL(string: urlString) {
// Create a URLSession data task
let task = URLSession.shared.dataTask(with: url) { data,
```

```
response, error in
// Check for errors if let error = error {
print("Error fetching data: \(error)")return
}

// Check for valid response and data
guard let httpResponse = response as?
HTTPURLResponse,
(200...299).contains(httpResponse.statusCode),
let data = data else { print("Invalid response or data.")
return
}

// Parse the JSON data

do {
if let jsonObject = try JSONSerialization.jsonObject(with:
data, options: []) as? [String: Any] { print("JSON
Response: \(jsonObject)")
}
} catch {
print("Error parsing JSON: \(error)")
}
}

// Start the network requesttask.resume()
}
```
```

### Explanation of the Code

**Creating a URL**: We create a `URL` object from a
string.
```

Creating Data Task: We use `URLSession.shared.dataTask(with:)` to initiate a network request. This function takes a URL and a completion handler that processes the response.

Handling the Response: We check for errors, validate the response, and parse the JSON data if everything is okay.

Starting the Task: Finally, we call `task.resume()` to start the request.### Making a POST Request

In addition to GET requests, you may need to send data to an API using a POST request. Here's how to do that:

```swift
let postURL = URL(string: "https://jsonplaceholder.typicode.com/posts")!    var request = URLRequest(url: postURL)
request.httpMethod = "POST"
request.setValue("application/json", forHTTPHeaderField: "Content-Type") let postData: [String: Any] = ["title": "foo", "body": "bar", "userId": 1]
do {
request.httpBody = try JSONSerialization.data(withJSONObject: postData, options: [])
} catch {
print("Error creating JSON: \(error)")return
}

let postTask = URLSession.shared.dataTask(with: request) { data, response, error iniflet error = error {
print("Error sending data: \(error)")return
}
```

```
guard    let    httpResponse    =    response    as?
HTTPURLResponse,
(200...299).contains(httpResponse.statusCode),
let data = data else { print("Invalid response or data.")
return

}

// Print out the response data
print("Response Data: \(String(data: data, encoding:
.utf8)!)")
}

postTask.resume()
```

Explanation of the POST Request Code

Prepare   the   URL   and   Request: Create   a
`URLRequest` object, set the HTTP method to "POST",
and set the `Content-Type` header.
Set the HTTP Body: Convert your data (dictionary)
into JSON using `JSONSerialization` and attach it to the
request's `httpBody`.
Handle Response: Similar to the GET request, check
for errors and handle the response appropriately.

Error Handling and Advanced Features

In real applications, it's important to handle errors
properly. Network requests can fail for many reasons,
including connectivity issues, server downtime, or invalid
responses. Swift offers robust error handling mechanisms.

Using `try-catch` Statements: This allows us to catch any issues that arise during JSON parsing or network requests.

Time Out and Request Configuration: `URLSessionConfiguration` allows you to set a timeout policy, cache policy, and additional settings tailored to your app's needs.

Background Networking: For tasks that take a longer time, you can utilize background sessions.

Authentication: Handle token-based authentication by setting the appropriate headers in your requests.

In this chapter, we explored how to make network requests in Swift using `URLSession`. We covered the basics of GET and POST requests, handling responses, and error management.

Parsing JSON Data

Swift, Apple's programming language for iOS, macOS, watchOS, and tvOS apps, provides sophisticated tools to handle JSON data seamlessly. This chapter will guide you through the essential steps and best practices for parsing JSON data in Swift.

Understanding JSON

Before diving into the code, let's briefly recap what JSON is. JSON is a lightweight data interchange format that's easy for humans to read and write and easy for machines to parse and generate. It consists of key-value pairs and can represent complex nested structures.

A simple JSON example looks like this:

```json
{
"name": "John Doe","age": 30, "isEmployed": true,
"skills": ["Swift", "Python", "JavaScript"],"address": {
"street": "123 Main St","city": "New York",
"state": "NY"
}
}
```

Parsing JSON in Swift ### Step 1: Creating a Model
The first step in parsing JSON is to define the structure of the data we expect. We will create a Swift model that matches the JSON structure. For our example above, we can define a struct as follows:

```swift
struct Address: Codable {let street: String
let city: String let state: String
}

struct User: Codable {let name: String
let age: Int
let isEmployed: Boollet skills: [String]
let address: Address
}
```

We are using the `Codable` protocol, which combines the

200

`Encodable` and `Decodable` protocols to simplify coding and decoding processes.

Step 2: Fetching JSON Data

Next, we'll fetch the JSON data, which could come from a web service or local file. For demonstration purposes, let's simulate fetching the data from a remote URL.

Here's a simple function to fetch the data asynchronously:

```swift
import Foundation

func fetchUserData(completion: @escaping (User?) -> Void) { guard let url = URL(string: "https://api.example.com/user") else {
print("Invalid URL")completion(nil) return
}

let task = URLSession.shared.dataTask(with: url) { data, response, error inguard let data = data, error == nil else {
print("Error fetching data: \(error?.localizedDescription ?? "No error info")")completion(nil)
return
}

do {
let user = try JSONDecoder().decode(User.self, from: data)completion(user)
} catch {
print("Error decoding JSON: \(error.localizedDescription)")completion(nil)
```

```
}
}

task.resume()
}
```

Step 3: Using the Parsed Data

Once we have successfully parsed the JSON into our Swift model, we can use it in our application. Below is an example of how to call the `fetchUserData` function and handle the result:

```swift
fetchUserData { user in guard let user = user else {
print("Failed to parse user data")return
}

print("User Name: \(user.name)") print("User Age: \(user.age)")

print("Is Employed: \(user.isEmployed)") print("Skills: \(user.skills.joined(separator: ","))")
print("Address: \(user.address.street), \(user.address.city), \(user.address.state)")
}
```

Error Handling

Error handling is a crucial aspect of working with JSON data. The above code captures errors at various points:

when fetching data, decoding JSON, and handling potential nil values. Swift's error handling capabilities make it easier to manage errors without crashing the application.

In this chapter, we explored the essential steps for parsing JSON data in Swift. We defined our data model using the `Codable` protocol, saw how to fetch JSON data using `URLSession`, and handled errors gracefully. Understanding these concepts is vital for any iOS or macOS developer who anticipates working with APIs or any data that comes in JSON format.

Conclusion

As we reach the end of "Swift App Development: Your First iOS App from Start to Finish," it's essential to reflect on the journey you've taken. From the first lines of code to the final touches that brought your app to life, you've acquired invaluable skills that will serve as the foundation for your future projects.

Throughout this book, we've navigated the essential

concepts of Swift programming, explored the intricacies of Xcode, and demystified the app development process. You've learned how to design user interfaces that are not only functional but also engaging, and you've gained insights into best practices for coding and debugging.

Remember, creating an app is more than just writing code; it's about understanding your users and delivering value through a seamless experience. As you continue to develop your skills, don't shy away from experimenting and pushing the boundaries of what you've learned. Each project you undertake will teach you something new and help you grow as a developer.

The world of iOS development is ever-evolving, and staying updated with the latest trends, tools, and best practices is crucial. Engage with the developer community, join forums, and participate in discussions to expand your knowledge and connect with other developers.

Your journey has just begun, and the skills you've gained in this ebook are only the beginning. Whether you pursue app development as a hobby or a career, embrace the challenges and celebrate your achievements.
Each app you create will enhance your understanding and expertise, bringing you one step closer to your next big project.

Thank you for allowing me to guide you through your first iOS app development experience. I hope you feel empowered to continue your learning and dive deeper into the exciting world of Swift and iOS development. The possibilities are endless, and with your newfound knowledge, you're well on your way to creating incredible applications that can impact users around the globe.

Happy coding, and best of luck on your future adventures in app development!

Biography

Oliver Snowden is an acclaimed author and tech enthusiast whose profound insights into Edward Snowden's life and legacy have captivated readers worldwide. With a rich background in web development and programming, Oliver brings a unique perspective to his writing, blending technical expertise with a deep understanding of the intricacies of privacy and surveillance in the digital age.

An advocate for transparency and digital freedom, Oliver has dedicated countless hours to researching and unraveling the complex narrative of Edward Snowden. His book offers a comprehensive and nuanced exploration of

Snowden's journey, shedding light on the pivotal moments that shaped his path and the implications of his actions on global privacy and security.

Beyond his passion for storytelling and tech advocacy, Oliver is an avid coder, specializing in Swift and web programming. He enjoys crafting innovative web applications that push the boundaries of what's possible in the digital realm. When he's not writing or coding, you can find him exploring the latest trends in web development, attending tech conferences, and sharing his knowledge with budding programmers through workshops and online tutorials.

Oliver's dedication to both his craft and his interests is evident in every page of his book, making it a must-read for anyone seeking to understand the man behind the headlines and the technological landscape that frames his story. Join Oliver Snowden on a journey of discovery, where the worlds of technology, privacy, and human courage intersect in the most inspiring ways.

Glossary: Swift App Development

A

API (Application Programming Interface)
A set of definitions and protocols used for building and integrating application software. APIs allow different software systems to communicate and interact with each other, providing developers with predefined functions to manage interactions with device hardware, data, or external services.

App Delegate
The central point of control in an iOS application. This object conforms to the `UIApplicationDelegate` protocol and responds to application-level events like launching, entering the background, and receiving notifications.

B

Backend
The server-side portion of an application responsible for managing data, performing computations, and handling business logic. It usually interacts with the frontend via APIs.

Build
The process of compiling source code into an executable form. In Xcode, builds can target different configurations (debug/release) and architectures.

C

Cocoa Touch
A UI framework for building iOS applications. It provides the necessary infrastructure for handling user interface elements, gestures, touch events, and more.

Closure
A self-contained block of functionality that can be passed around and used in your code. Closures can capture and store references to variables and constants from the context in which they are defined.

D

Delegate
A design pattern in Swift that enables one object to communicate back to another. The delegate handles events or actions, providing a way for one class to delegate functionality to another without tight coupling.

Dependency Injection
A design pattern in which an object receives its dependencies from an external source rather than creating them internally. This promotes modularity and enhances testability.

E

Enum (Enumeration)
A data type that consists of a group of related values. Enums in Swift are powerful and can have associated values and methods, enabling more expressive coding practices.

Error Handling
A mechanism in Swift for managing and responding to runtime errors. It involves using `do`, `try`, and `catch` keywords to handle exceptions systematically.##
F
Framework
A structured collection of code, libraries, and resources that provide specific functionalities to applications. Frameworks can be built-in (like UIKit) or third-party.

Function
A self-contained block of code that performs a specific task and may return a value. Functions help organize code and promote reusability.

G

Git
A version control system used to track changes in code during development. It allows multiple developers to collaborate effectively by managing codes' history and versions.

GCD (Grand Central Dispatch)
A low-level API for managing concurrent tasks in iOS applications. GCD helps optimize application performance through efficient execution of tasks in parallel or asynchronously.

H

Hyperlink
A reference to data that the user can follow by clicking.

This term is mostly applicable to web applications, but can also pertain to linking screens or content in an app.

I

IBOutlet
An interface builder outlet in Swift. It allows you to connect UI components from the storyboard directly to your source code, enabling programmatic control of user interface elements.

IBAction
An interface builder action in Swift that allows you to connect user interface components (e.g., buttons) to event handlers in your code. When the user interacts with the UI element, the corresponding method is executed.

J

JSON (JavaScript Object Notation)
A lightweight data-interchange format that is easy for humans to read and write and easy for machines to parse and generate. JSON is widely used to transmit data between server and client in web applications.

K

Key-Value Coding (KVC)
A mechanism that allows you to access object properties indirectly using strings to refer to property names. This provides flexible and dynamic ways of accessing an object's attributes.

L

Lazy Variables
Properties in Swift that are not initialized until they are first accessed. This feature is useful for saving memory by delaying the creation of complex objects until they are really needed.

M

Model-View-Controller (MVC)
A design pattern used to separate an application into three interconnected components: the Model (data), the View (UI), and the Controller (business logic). This separation improves modularity and code manageability.

Module
A self-contained unit of code that encapsulates related functions, types, and assets. Modules improve code organization and reuse across different applications.

N

Network Call
A request made from a client application to a server to retrieve or send data over the internet. In Swift, network calls can be made using `URLSession`.

O

IBOutletCollection
An array of outlets that references a collection of UI elements. This allows for organized manipulation of

multiple UI components within a single entity.

Optional
A type that can hold either a value or `nil`, signifying the absence of a value. Optionals in Swift enable safer handling of data and prevent runtime crashes.

P

Pod
A library or module that can be integrated into a Swift project using CocoaPods, a dependency manager for Cocoa projects.

Protocol
A blueprint of methods, properties, and other requirements that suit a particular task or piece of functionality. Protocols define what methods a class must implement without providing the implementation details.

Q

Query
A request for information or data from a database or a data source. In the context of apps, querying is often done through network APIs.

R

Repository
A storage location for code, usually associated with source control systems like Git. A repository contains all the files, code history, and tracking information.

S

SwiftUI
A modern framework for building user interfaces across all Apple platforms. SwiftUI leverages a declarativesyntax, enabling developers to create intuitive and dynamic UIs effortlessly.

Singleton
A design pattern that restricts a class to a single instance and provides a global point of access to that instance. Singletons are often used for shared resources.

T

Test Flight
An Apple service used to distribute beta applications to testers for feedback and issues before the finalrelease. It allows developers to manage builds and gather insights from users.

Tuple
A group of multiple values or items that are stored together. Tuples are useful for returning multiple results from a function or organizing related data.

U

UIKit
A framework used for constructing and managing a graphical user interface in iOS applications. UIKitprovides the structure and functionality for views, controls, and

animations.

V

View Controller
An object that manages a portion of your app's user interface. View controllers handle user interactions, manage the views, and coordinate communication between them.

W

Xcode
Apple's integrated development environment (IDE) for macOS used for developing applications on Apple platforms. Xcode includes a code editor, debugging tools, and UI design capabilities.

Workflow
The sequence of tasks that a developer follows during the development process. Effective workflows improve productivity and maintain quality.

Y

YAML (YAML Ain't Markup Language)
A human-readable data serialization standard often used for configuration files. YAML is sometimes used in Swift projects for easier readability and configuration management.

Z

Zeroing Weak Reference
In Swift, a weak reference that automatically becomes nil when the object it references is deallocated. This helps prevent retain cycles and memory leaks.